Begg to

Ally Begg

Foreword by Sir Alex Ferguson CBE

Rudling House Publishing Limited,
Kemp House, 152 City Road, London EC1V 2NX

© Ally Begg 2014

Published in the UK in 2014 by Rudling House.
A CIP catalogue record for this book is available
from the British Library.

Typeset in Sabon by www.julietdoyle.com
Cover design by www.paineproffitt.com

ISBN: 978-0-9562760-4-9
www.rudlinghouse.com

Printed and bound by CPI Group (UK) Ltd, Croydon, CR0 4YY

ii

Contents

Dedication

This book is dedicated to my late father, John Begg, and grandpa, John Begg, who simply were the greatest dad and grandpa anybody could ever have – I miss you both every day

Foreword

It is a pleasure to do the Foreword for Ally Begg's book on his journey as a lifetime Aberdeen FC fan. Anyone brought up in that era must have a million stories to tell. Of course there will always be plenty of myth and embellishments of events of that time but it is in Ally's experience as a media man to separate the facts from the fiction. It is quite easy to look back and wonder how it was all done, even for me when I look back at those years, I realise it was some sort of miracle.

A Scottish team built in the Granite City, all Scottish born, the oldest player was around 27, goes to Gothenburg and beats the mighty Real Madrid. Di Stefano says after the game that they couldn't beat the spirit of Aberdeen, praise indeed. However that was only the culmination of some serious progress before the emergence of that squad of players had laid down their mark by usurping the power of the Old Firm. Yes, heady days for the Aberdeen fans. How could it all have happened?

Well I am sure there will be many reasons to read about it and for Aberdeen fans another opportunity to drift back into the memory of all their achievements. This is bound to be a good read so enjoy it as I'm looking forward to it myself.

Sir Alex Ferguson CBE

Acknowledgements

A big thank you to my family past and present who helped inspire this book, my good friends Craig Coughlan, Richard Wilkinson and Harry Brooks, who looked over the early transcripts and offered invaluable advice. My editor, Dan Tester, who brought the book to life and who showed remarkable patience with one who struggled to even get an English "O" grade at school.

Thank you to everyone at Rudling House Publishers, but a special mention must go to Karen Butler who believed in the project and had the foresight to encourage me to finish it.

Sincere thanks must go to my wife Miriam who offered nothing but the very best support throughout the final few months. The late nights, the throwing of pens, the bashing of computers and the occasional swear word has all been forgiven!

And finally, to all Aberdonians everywhere, this book is for you!

Picture acknowledgements

All photos taken from Ally Begg's personal collection ©Ally Begg with the following exceptions:

Bad Boys Inc photos ©Julian Barton, Bad Boys Inc official photographer

Modelling photos ©Ray Smith at Ray Smith Photography

Introduction

Whether we like it or not, life is about trials and tribulations. We form our own paths and follow our own destiny. I believe fate plays its hand here and there but, ultimately, we choose where we go in life. We are in charge and we make decisions which shape the meaning of our own existence. Life is a journey – an adventure!

I have tried my damnedest not to turn this book into an autobiography as, let's be honest, who am I to do such a thing? This book is my journey through life, from childhood to adulthood. My adventure, though, has been the catalyst for my life – Aberdeen Football Club!

I have been blessed to lead a life that some can only dream of, but I wanted to use the pages of this book to inspire those who want more. If I can do it, then anybody can. I thank my lucky stars to have lived such a varied and exciting existence so far but the one common denominator, the one constant companion throughout my life has, and always will be, my absolute love and fierce passion for Aberdeen Football Club.

From the early 1980s to the present day I have told all my stories. Success in the early days was part of the norm. In my adulthood I have forgotten what it's like to taste that success. I crave it, I need it, but I doubt I will see it on that level ever again. Players who I loved, players who I despised, games that I will never forget, games that I want to forget but can't.

Like all Aberdeen fans of my generation I look back on the grand old days with fondness and pride. It's all here on these pages.

After many years searching, I have found my chosen profession and find myself extremely fortunate to love the job

I do. It's offered me the opportunity to enjoy the company of those that I once idolised. I have met childhood heroes and forged close friendships with players whom I admired as a youngster. Like millions before me my path has been fraught with different challenges. I have faced them all head on and believe, after some serious soul searching and questioning of one's sanity, I have come through it a stronger and better person. From humble beginnings in Newburgh, where I grew up, to the bright lights of London where my path unintentionally shifted, and on to the Far East where my life began to take shape, I have never given up, even when faced with adversity and absurdity.

I would like to share the adventure with you ...

Scottish League Cup Final – 2014

For a moment, the sun poked its head out from the dark grey clouds high above Celtic Park to have a look at what all the fuss was about. I put my arm on my brother Peter's shoulder and whispered into his ear that Dad "is looking down on us". Peter gently bowed his head, turned and smiled gently back at me without speaking. All around us, 40,000 fellow Aberdeen fans filled Scotland's finest stadium hoping to see Aberdeen lift a trophy for the first time in 19 years. I believed there and then as I caught the warmth of the sun's rays on my face that victory would be ours. Like Peter, I gently bowed my head and remembered my late father who had been so cruelly taken away from us seven years previously. Dad loved occasions like this, as did Mum, and I so wish he could have been here in body, not spirit, to watch the events unfold. Whilst lost in those thoughts the remainder of the game passed me by. Before I knew it I was looking up to the heavens again asking Dad to make sure that all Aberdeen players scored their respective penalty kicks ahead of the dreaded shoot-out after a drab 0–0 draw over 120 minutes.

Ironically, I sensed victory could be ours in the competition the night Aberdeen so nearly crashed out to Alloa Athletic. The Scottish Championship outfit frustrated the home side all evening until the Dons prevailed 6-5 in another penalty shoot-out. For the next game I watched the Dons tear Falkirk apart quite magnificently from my hotel room in Doha, on Aberdeen's very own internet TV service RED TV, before another superlative performance saw the boys beat much-fancied Motherwell 2–0 at Fir Park in the quarter-finals. At this stage of the competition I started to wonder if Aberdeen had enough in their locker to go all the way to the final. When Aberdeen were paired with St Johnstone for the semi-final, I said to my Austrian wife Miriam that we should book our flight home for the week of the final. She shrugged as if I had just spoken to her in Chinese and agreed! Get in! For the semi-final I finished off a busy day in the office by getting home in plenty of time for kick-off. Being three hours ahead of the UK meant juggling bath time with my baby son Lennox, helping Miriam prepare dinner and keeping my PC forever in eye shot while going about my fatherly and husbandly duties! For the first time in many years my mood was one of serenity as kick-off approached. This was a different team, a different era from the sides that had failed so miserably in the previous five semi-finals in the more recent past. I felt quietly optimistic that another cup final would beckon our doors once again, my first since the turn of the new millennium – where had the time gone! God, I'm not getting any younger! The ref blew his whistle, the game was underway. Lennox, who only the day before took his first steps much to the excitement of his Mum and I, was testing out his new-found skill which for a moment diverted my attention away from the game. Looking like a newborn foal trying to stand for the first time, I looked on in some amusement as Lennox stumbled to his feet – his wee bottom sticking out for all to see! In that precise moment the match commentator's words caught my attention: "Adam Rooney could be in here, he's got plenty of support in the middle – Steven Anderson leaves it – Aberdeen are in front, it's Jonny Hayes." I looked up to see young Mr Hayes running away from goal in celebration! "Holy shit we've scored." Aberdeen had taken the lead in only the third minute of the game! I checked Lennox, all fine, looked back at my PC, Aberdeen fans going crazy, looked at Miriam, she laughed, looked back at Lennox, HE SMILED! He's an Aberdeen fan already!!!! This was turning out to be a good day!

As the game settled after a brilliant start by Aberdeen, I decided bath time should be done quickly, yet effectively. Lennox was bathed and changed within the blink of an eye, his bath water transformed into a foam, such was the speed of his scrub from top to bottom. His all-in-one pyjamas, thrown on with such skill he didn't even have time to question his attire for the night. Mickey Mouse would simply have to do! All the while I conveyed strict instructions to Miriam to get his bottle ready as I was not messing around. With bottle in one hand, favourite teddy in the other, I offered a goodnight kiss and one last look of love before jogging back to the living room to watch the remainder of the game.

Bedtime had been timed to perfection because just as I took my seat Jonny Hayes crossed an inviting ball into the penalty area from the left flank, the ball broke to young Peter Pawlett on the edge of the box who proceeded to skip past his immediate opponent and bore down on goal. At this stage I was back on my feet trying to keep my voice to its minimum volume conscious the wee one was trying to sleep next door. "Go on son, go on my son – yeeeeeessssssss!!!!!" Aberdeen had scored a second! I was jumping up and down in my living room enjoying the moment at home just as much as the travelling support at Tynecastle. Surely now we had too much for St Johnstone, surely now we can go and hold on, surely now we can make it to the cup final???

With half-time came scenes of joy from the Begg household. I skipped into the bathroom where Miriam had now taken occupancy of the bath trying to relax knowing her husband was only a few feet away shaking with nervous tension! At least one of us could afford to chill out! I told her if all things worked out well we could make the final. While we were home maybe, just maybe, her dad Sigi would like to come along and sample the might of Scottish football for the first time? "Sounds like a nice idea," she said. I had her in the palm of my hand – I knew there and then I was going to the final! I prayed the Dons, though, would not capitulate in the second half. All fears were put to bed just after the half-hour mark when Peter Pawlett stole the ball in the middle of the park, played a delightfully weighted ball to new signing Adam Rooney, who bore down on goal and slotted home as easy as you like. Once again I was up on my feet jumping up and down like a demented lunatic, much to the amusement of one's wife, who had not seen her husband celebrate an Aberdeen goal in such a manner before. The peculiar look on her face will stay with me for a while! As the Red Army celebrated wildly, I had to continue my celebrations on mute. You can only but trust me when I tell you celebrating quietly is not an easy task given the circumstances I found myself in! 3–0, game over! At last, I could sit back and relax and enjoy the rest of the game! When Jonny Hayes added a delightfully crafted solo goal with ten minutes to go I went looking for the cigars! What a game, what a performance, what a result! We had made it!

Please allow me to skip forward a couple of weeks to when we arrived back home after an exhausting overnight trip from Qatar. I could sense the excitement building...

All local media – newspapers, radio, television and social media – concentrated their efforts on offering the very best service in the build-up to the big game. Everywhere I went folk had one topic on their mind; the League Cup Final! This was different from before, in the 1980s this was part of the norm, which I will expand on later in the book, but in the year 2014 the sense of the occasion could not escape me. I was completely wrapped up in it. This almost felt like my first ever cup final, even though I had watched Aberdeen triumph in all but the two previous finals since 1981. On the Thursday before the game, I made my way to Pittodrie Stadium to meet up with media manager and good friend, Malcolm Panton, who had kindly arranged my tickets. Sat in his office chatting away, I really started to feel almost childlike, excited beyond belief as he handed me my tickets. Here I was, 41-years-old, feeling like a 12-year-old! I called Peter and told him I had possession of the tickets, to which he gave out a loud "hurrah". We both could not wait for Sunday! When the big day eventually arrived, I felt remarkably calm. I enjoyed my breakfast and skimmed through the morning newspapers like any other normal day yet I knew, subconsciously, this was not a normal day. I guess my preoccupation with looking after Lennox and making sure my in-laws – who do not speak English – felt comfortable in their Scottish surroundings, afforded my mind to relax from thinking about the football. I was delighted Sigi, my father-in-law, was coming with us as our bond is strong, even if the obvious language barrier holds us back somewhat from having a normal relationship. I knew from his body language he was looking forward to the game just as much as I was. Peter was picked up from the airport without too much fuss, as were the hordes of Aberdeen fans who made their way up from the capital city. Glasgow Airport suddenly becoming a sea of red and white!

With every passing minute, the excitement levels rose just that little bit more. My uncle Bill very kindly offered to drive us down to Celtic Park which, believe me, saved much hassle on my part having to, one, remember how to get there and, two, find a decent car-parking space without some wee ned asking for a fiver to look after my car! As we neared the stadium I could hear "Stand free wherever you may be, we are the famous Aberdeen" rise from the back streets of the east end of Glasgow, the volume getting louder with each passing second. Just then, like a Hollywood movie scene, a cast of thousands met our eyes as the Aberdeen fans marched their way to Celtic Park. It took my breath away, what a view! The volume of singing was now deafening – Sigi was speechless. I doubt he had witnessed anything like this in his life before. In that moment I wanted to jump out the car and join the march, I wanted to feel a part of the cast, I wanted to sing my heart out without worrying about hitting a bum note or sounding out of tune! I wanted a starring role in this scene, but conscious of my uncle's efforts, I stayed put and enjoyed the procession from the relative comfort of his car. Having been dropped off safely we walked the short distance to the stadium, stopping only once to buy an Aberdeen scarf for Sigi! From every angle, Aberdeen fans swarmed around us, thousands upon thousands of happy faces all looking forward to the game. Upon entering the stadium I was met with what can only be described as a sea of colour – all red and white! It was simply awe-inspiring! I had been to Celtic Park on a European night for Celtic's Champions League games and the sight that meets one's eyes raises the hairs on the back of your neck, but this was different. This was my team, my fellow fans all here for one common purpose, to see Aberdeen hopefully win the League Cup. My heart was racing as kick-off approached. Nineteen years, 19 bloody long years, but at last the ref blew his whistle and we were off!

120 minutes came and went without any scoring. I took one last look at the heavens, asked Dad to do his best to help the boys, clenched my fists to my chest, took a deep breath and watched Inverness Caley Thistle's Billy McKay step up to take the first penalty. I was huddled behind Sigi and Peter but had enough of a vantage point to see the entire penalty area. The noise all around me was deafening, then a hush as McKay began his run-up, in the flash of an eye Jamie Langfield, Aberdeen's hero all season, dived to his right and saved magnificently. All around me erupted; I simply jumped up and down! Oh my God here we go as Aberdeen's Barry Robson took the long walk to the penalty spot. I closed my eyes for a second, looked back and GOOAAAALLLL! I jumped up and down again – this time a little faster than before.

Thistle's Greg Tansey was next in the queue for Inverness, "miss it" I shouted "MISS IT" then lo and behold he put his penalty so far over the bar the ball almost ended up outside Celtic Park. Once again all around me went crazy, I jumped up and down, this time making inane noises! We had a major advantage now. Surely to Christ we won't blow it from here? Young Nicky Low was next for the Dons and his short run-up made me nervous but he blasted the ball low into the corner of the net – GOOOAAALLLL! Aberdeen were now 2–0 in front! "Holy crap, I think we're going to do it," I said to Peter, who was too busy grinning to reply! Nick Ross kept his cool for Inverness, as did Scott Vernon for Aberdeen. I sensed we had a hand on the trophy, I sensed we had done enough. I sensed Dad was working his magic from high above! Aaron Dorran kept his composure for Inverness and he scored. Aberdeen led 3–2, but we all knew if Adam Rooney scored the next penalty Aberdeen would win the cup!

I can't begin to describe to you, on paper, what it feels like in that two or three minutes between penalty kicks. Everybody around me double-checked with each other that if Rooney scored Aberdeen would win the cup. Everyone concurred and then, for a fleeting moment, a hush descended over the Aberdeen end. I looked down then up to the heavens one last time, I shifted my weight, held my hands to my mouth, closed my eyes, then settled. Rooney began his run-up and... GOOAAAAALLLLLLLLLLLLL! He had slotted his penalty high into the net and Celtic Park exploded! I have no shame in telling you I went a little nuts screaming "yes, yes, yes" at the top of my voice, while punching through the night air! Oh my good lord in heaven, we had won the cup. I grabbed Peter and held him tight, Sigi grabbed us both and Peter and I embraced him like we would have done with our own Dad. All three of us shared a magical moment together! I swear in that moment I almost started crying! What a moment and what a bloody way to win a cup final!

Unbelievable scenes greeted us as we composed ourselves. Celtic Park was bouncing with Aberdeen fans literally going nuts. The players on the pitch did likewise. It really was fantastic to watch as all around us celebrated a famous cup win. When Russell Anderson stepped forward to lift the trophy Peter and I stood shoulder to shoulder and grinned like Cheshire cats as the ticker tape exploded into the night sky! What a great moment and what a great trip!

At the time of writing, Aberdeen are on the crest of a wave, enjoying a season like none other in many a year. There is a buzz, not just about Pittodrie, but about the city and the surrounding areas that at long last maybe, just maybe, Derek McInnes and his coaching staff are building a side that can challenge Celtic and offer us, the success-starved fans, something to not just look forward to, but to cheer as well. It's been a horrendous time for the club post-Sir Alex Ferguson days, but we are seeing light at the end of a very long tunnel. From a personal point of view, I have not shared this type of emotion since I was a kid. It is strange now, as a man, husband and father, how I feel about my club again. I look forward to every game. I arrange my schedule in and around games so I don't miss out! Honestly, I am like a big kid at times and I'm loving it. But, you have to trust me when I tell you it's been hell over the past 25 years or so. Allow me then to take you right back to the beginning, to fully understand why football has played a major role throughout my life.

Born to be a Dandy Don

I'm not going to bore you with a typical autobiographical beginning to a book. Why would you give a shit where I was born, what school I went to, and what I was like as a child before I discovered football? Let's cut to the chase and get straight to the point of this tome. Football is in my blood; it's been passed down the Begg family for generations. My grandpa, John Begg, was a freelance football journalist based in Glasgow and my uncle Bill Marwick, up until he retired recently, was also a journalist who specialised in the lower leagues. Both men are hugely respected throughout the game, men of honour and integrity. I am yet to hear a bad word about either from anyone involved in the game.

Legend states that in 1974 the former St Mirren chairman Willie Todd called my grandpa and asked him for his advice as he was seeking a new manager. My grandpa offered Mr Todd one name, Alex Ferguson! You will hear many a tale about my grandpa in this book and I make no apology for it; he was my hero and left a huge void in my life when he died in 1990. I would like to think that I have carried on his and Bill's legacy in my own career.

I must say at this stage I have dropped one or two names from the world of sport and showbusiness. The intention is not to be smug or clever, or even arrogant, but unfortunately – or fortunately – depending which side of the fence you sit on, these "celebs" have somehow played a role in my life. I implore you not to judge me on the dropped names. I do not have any celebrity friends, nor do I feel the need to have any.

It makes me very proud that my true friends are those who I have known all my life, or a significant part of it.

My Dad was always a football fanatic. From a very young age he supported Clyde and it was not uncommon for him to accompany my grandpa into many a press box. It was also not unusual to see him taking notes on a game while grandpa was busy at home clattering away on his typewriter. A quick jump on the train or tram from Glasgow took Dad to many a ground where members of the press looked after him. Dad had no interest in journalism and I have no doubt his love for all things planes, trains and trams was born from travelling to football grounds the length and breadth of Scotland during the 1950s and early 1960s. You can see then, that my understanding and love for the game was built on strong foundations.

His behaviour, language, demeanour and passion for football helped mould my own love for the sport from a very young age. He only "lost it" twice in my lifetime and, from what I can remember, both were comical to the core. The first experience I will never forget!

I was five years old. It was late one night and I was in bed, but not asleep. I heard a yell from downstairs, which gave me a scare. I wondered what it was and climbed out of bed and stood at the top of the stairs sucking on my comfort blanket. My little brother Peter was fast asleep in his bed; in one month he would be three years old. I made my way down the stairs and into the living room where Mum picked me up and placed me on her knee while Dad continued to watch this game on TV that I recognised immediately. I had played this game with my Dad in the back garden but this was different. More people, big stadium, lots of noise and so much colour. My Dad looked excited and slightly odd, as he kept moving up and down in his chair; he looked over at me a couple of times and winked. I smiled back. Mum held me tight.

Then my Dad was on his feet with eyes bulging. I was bewildered, slightly alarmed and wondering, what's all this? What it was was a bit of history. Then he yelled at the top of his voice "What a goal, Christ; what a GOAL. My God... Did you SEE THAT? DID – YOU – SEE – THAT?" This was the first football match I had ever seen. And, though I didn't know it at the time, we had just watched a legend being born. It was June 11th 1978. Scotland were playing Holland in the World Cup, and Archie Gemmill had just snaked through the penalty area to score his sensational solo effort. Today, it's ranked as the sixth best goal of all time — and it was the first one I had ever seen. Some start to a fan's career, eh? To use that dreadfully over-exposed word "awesome" this was aweSOME.

I've never seen a better goal (well, maybe Ryan Giggs' FA Cup semi-final effort against Arsenal in 1999 and more recently Zlatan Ibrahimovic's stunning bicycle kick against England) but in my current job as a TV sports producer, one way and another, I've seen a lot of football and lots of goals and Archie's is still one of the best I have ever seen. One of the interesting aspects about Gemmill's goal is that, for my family at least, it was sort of disconnected from Scotland. We were actually living in Holland at the time as my Dad was working for an aviation company near Maastricht. So it's probably a good job I was only five. If I had been more grown-up I would probably have got into a few playground bundles with my Dutch friends!

Another aspect that interests me now in my current role is how we would treat that goal on TV today. Apart from the fact that TV screens were only about 21 inches back then, and there was no HD, the coverage was very basic by comparison to today. Six cameras covered that match, like most others back in 1978. Today, Sky would use 14, including at least one steady-cam on the touchline. Add to that super slow motion! So, can you imagine the treatment that goal would have received from a host of sports broadcasters? They would have reviewed it over and over from every angle, and at almost one frame at a time. We have diagrams to explain in detail the defensive lapses. We would measure his speed through the box, how near the defenders' feet came to him, how close he kept the ball to his own feet. How long it all took... In fact, it was remarkably quick, only about four seconds.

Gemmill would have been interviewed to death. The managers would have been interviewed to death. The opponents would have been interviewed to death. The fans – in fact, anybody with the slightest connection to the team; from the boot boy, to the coach driver! It's what I love about TV and how we cover sport. It's obscenely over-the-top and "Hollywood" but that is what has made football the animal it is today. I feel very lucky to be working in an industry that offers me the opportunity to talk about the game I love on a daily basis.

A year on from that glorious evening watching Dad lose the plot, he moved our family to Aberdeen, Scotland to begin a brand new marketing and commercial job with a small aviation company based out of Aberdeen Airport. Aberdeen FC were still unknown to me at the time but it wasn't long before my life as a Dons fan began. Dad continued to watch football on TV and he allowed me to watch with him, unless it was very late. Before school at the breakfast table he would read the back page of the local newspaper, the *Press & Journal* and wax lyrical about the local football team who, only months before, had been crowned champions of Scotland.

He talked about going to this place called Pittodrie – and taking me with him – but it would be a good 12 months before he actually did. Up until then I had to be content with watching football on TV. Before the Dons, I remember watching Arsenal losing the 1980 Cup Winners' Cup Final against Valencia on penalties. Dad told me, I cried, and threw a tantrum! Unknown to me at the time the Cup Winners' Cup and Arsenal would play a major role in my life in years to come. I became a fully-fledged "dandy" when Aberdeen played Austria Memphis (now Vienna) in the European Cup. I felt excited about my local team playing in the competition my Dad had told me so much about.

If I heard the story of him attending the 1960 European Cup Final with my grandpa at Hampden between Real Madrid and Eintracht Frankfurt once, I heard it a million times. The match against Memphis at Pittodrie was, of course, a very special occasion and I had to wait until the morning after the night before to find out the result. The Dons won 1–0 thanks to a goal from Mark McGhee. I read the report in the paper and went to school feeling very happy.

I have no idea why I felt so happy exactly. This was a new emotion for me but it worked, it felt good. I've always wondered why young boys and girls fall in love with football clubs. Could it be a family connection, carrying on a parent's legacy perhaps? Is there a mysterious ingredient which is simply too difficult to explain on paper? I honestly don't know why I became an Aberdeen fan. I suppose it just felt right. All I know is from that moment on, the Dons were my team.

In the second round of the 1980/81 European competition, the Dons were paired with Liverpool. The two games presented a whole new set of emotions. I was eight-years-old and fully settled into our new life in Scotland. I was enjoying school, playing football and making new friends. Newburgh was growing as a village as more and more families moved into our newly built estate. I was still a few months away from my first game at Pittodrie. The arrival of Liverpool gripped the city; it was the talk of the town and it was impossible not to notice the excitement.

Unfortunately, I don't have memories of the first leg at Pittodrie but I clearly recall the away leg at Anfield and the confusion I felt when Dad woke me to the news that the Dons had been well-beaten 4–0. Aberdeen didn't lose by such a margin; this wasn't supposed to happen. I wasn't prepared for feeling so low due to a football match. Dad explained to me over breakfast that this was all part of supporting a club and to expect more disappointments. I sulked into my Rice Krispies, cursing the snap, crackle and bloody pop! Over the next few months I followed the team via the newspapers and match highlights on TV. I became familiar with the players and the manager Alex Ferguson. I knew the players by name and recognised them instantly. I had my favourites in the early days, like Peter Weir, Willie Miller and Gordon Strachan.

My first-ever game though, was not Aberdeen at Pittodrie but Scotland at Hampden Park. The date: 24th May 1980; the occasion, a home international against the Auld Enemy England. The score a 2–0 defeat. I wanted more of this excitement, noise, banter, atmosphere and colour and I wanted it no more than at Pittodrie where I wanted to sample the sights, smells and, as any Aberdeen fan will tell you, the seagulls!

After a whole year of persuasion and good behaviour Dad relented and took me to my first Aberdeen game. Mum bought me a brand new red scarf especially for the momentous occasion and wrapped me up tight. My excitement was bubbling over. I was up early and ready for my debut with the Scottish Premier Division. The 2nd May 1981 is where it all began and the last game of the 1980/81 season against Kilmarnock. We sat in the Main Stand and I clearly remember Dad lifting me over the turnstile (a feat he would do many times again) as we made our way in. What hit me first was how small Pittodrie felt; being at Hampden for my first game gave me a sense of large terraces with thousands of faces swarming around. That day ahead of kick-off, Pittodrie was almost empty and I felt a tad disappointed. I was hoping for atmosphere, colour and many more fans; alas it didn't turn out that way as the game against Kilmarnock was meaningless. I took my seat beside Dad and tucked into my sausage roll and skimmed through the pictures of the players in the matchday programme. Kick-off was moments away and I couldn't wait!

The team facing Kilmarnock that Saturday afternoon was:

Jim Leighton
Stuart Kennedy
Doug Rougvie
Andy Watson
Alex McLeish
Willie Miller
Neil Simpson
Mark McGhee
Joe Harper
Ian Angus
John Hewitt

The Dons lost 2–0! I did not expect this and it hurt. By their own standards the Dons did not play well that day and struggled against a team who ultimately were relegated to the First Division. I did not enjoy my Dons debut; thankfully this was one of very few defeats I would taste during my childhood as an Aberdeen fan. From then, my life at a relatively young age led me down a path, which ultimately turned into an obsession. Football, I decided, would become my life.

During the summer my understanding of all things football started to take shape. Reading the newspapers and watching the daily news offered me the chance to take my new-found love to a different level. I pestered Dad on more than one occasion for answers to why Ian Scanlon had left the club and why Peter Weir joined? Why on earth would anyone want to leave the Dons? Who was I to know at the time that Peter Weir would go on to become a firm favourite of mine? After what seemed like an eternity, season 1981/82 kicked off against Dundee United, a game I was very much looking forward to. For away games Dad always had the radio on in the background while Peter and I went about our Saturday afternoon business, be it cleaning up, mowing the lawn, washing the car or making *Star Wars* come to life with our toy figurines.

But come 3pm Luke Skywalker and co would have to wait for a couple of hours to save the galaxy. Light sabers were downed, peace was made with the Dark Side and I took my seat at the kitchen table to listen to BBC Radio Scotland. I wasn't really prepared for what happened next. The Dons had been thrashed 4–1! Oh well, back to saving the galaxy!

That season Dad started taking me to Pittodrie on a regular basis. At school on a Monday morning our teacher asked us to write a diary of our weekend. This was a simple task, a precise account of my afternoon watching the Dons, from the moment we arrived at Pittodrie to the second we left. This would continue for the next three years...

Even when asked by my teachers to tell a different tale, I had nothing else to say! For my ninth birthday Mum asked me what I would like as a present. She knew fine well what I wanted, a full Aberdeen home kit, of course! My first one! I needed no excuse to wear the kit at every opportunity. Mum had to drag it off me kicking and screaming just to wash it. I now felt like a proper football fan and my new-found hobby was just about to get so much better in the following months when the Scottish Cup started, my first taste of success as a Dandy Don.

From my first Scottish final back in 1982, to my last in the year 2000, I have only missed one: the 1993 Scottish Cup Final against Rangers at Celtic Park. At the time I had just signed a five-album record deal with A&M Records and was a tad preoccupied with learning how to sing and dance! I apologise for throwing this explanation in at such an early stage, and I will talk about this crazy part of my life a little later in the book but as valid reasons for missing a cup final go I think it's a pretty good one!

The Scottish Cup had always played a huge part in my Dad's life and he loved attending Hampden to re-live his own youth. The season after the Dons lost to Celtic in 1954, Clyde won the cup after beating the Hoops in a replay. The manager of Clyde at the time was a gentleman called Paddy Travers, the former Dons legend who was a friend of my grandpa's. In the immediate aftermath of the 1955 final, Mr Travers asked my grandpa if he would mind serving as keeper of the famous old trophy for a night due to the excessive celebrations the Clyde players had in mind after the victory. My grandpa duly obliged and took the Scottish Cup home with him. The day after my Dad celebrated his tenth birthday the very same trophy took pride of place on his sideboard in his small bedroom as he slept. Who would have known that almost fifty years later to the very day, his eldest son would take possession of the trophy for a special cup final show on Celtic TV, where I worked at the time.

My grandpa always used his magic to get us our cup final tickets; he pulled a few strings and cashed in some favours from various folk he knew in the game. Unfortunately for us, the tickets were always in the old Main Stand, in the opposing fans' section! For the first few years we had to be content with the company of Rangers, Celtic and Hearts supporters. By the time the 1982 Scottish Cup Final campaign commenced, I was already a devoted Don. My bedroom walls were covered with posters of the team and individual players. Flags, pennants and scarves hung from every nook and cranny; even my carpet was red! As a kid my Mum and Dad subscribed to *Shoot* magazine. Every year it contained a brand new double-page spread of the official team photograph and I couldn't wait to stick it up on my wall.

Removing the page was done with such precision it was almost military-like. Firstly, the tricky little staples had to be removed, my hands shaking in fear of ripping the paper. Secondly, I had to detach the sheet from the staples without making the holes any bigger or disfiguring the face of one of my heroes. A prime position on the wall was then chosen; perhaps a few other items had to be pushed to the side but eventually I was ready for the finale. Finding the smallest thumb pins (they had to be red, of course), I carefully pressed one corner into the wall, then the next corner making sure it was perfectly straight and pleasant on the eye. Come to think of it, a spirit level would have been very handy during my teens! Once the project was complete, I would sit back and admire my handiwork.

En route to the 1982 Scottish Cup Final Aberdeen played Celtic at Pittodrie in the fourth round. Sitting in the Main Stand with my folks, I remember the fans around us feeling uneasy with the team selection. Fergie had selected big Alex McLeish to play in midfield with Doug Rougvie moving to centre-back. However, it was obviously an inspired move as a solitary John Hewitt header was enough to progress to the quarter-finals. After beating Kilmarnock, the Dons faced St Mirren at Celtic Park in the semis. Unfortunately, the first game finished 1–1. From my point of view this was not good as the replay was scheduled for a Wednesday night – a school night. Early to bed was compulsory in those days so a cunning plan was devised to sneak a radio into my bedroom. A sound bollocking was also dished out when my excitement got the better of me after Peter Weir scored the winner in a tense 3–2 victory. I was overjoyed, over the moon, and I wanted to go to my first-ever Scottish Cup Final.

The next morning at breakfast, I read the match report in the *Press & Journal* and asked Dad if we could go to the final to watch the Dons take on the might of Rangers. I think he was always prepared for this type of question, as he would always retort with a "we'll see". Thinking back, this was a rather ingenious ploy because it wasn't quite a "yes" but more importantly it wasn't a "no". When he told me a few weeks later we were going, I was overcome with excitement. We drove down to Glasgow after school on the Friday night, Dad managing to get away early from work. We always stayed in Bishopbriggs, a suburb just to the north of Glasgow, with my gran and grandpa. I loved cup final mornings. I'd go through all the papers grandpa had bought, reading the complimentary pull-outs and watching the early build-up on TV. Before setting off for south Glasgow lunch would be served by gran; a feast fit for a king and enough to keep us all going for the afternoon ahead. The day of the game, 22nd May 1982, was beautiful with the sun high in the sky. We travelled to Hampden in plenty of time as grandpa had to arrive early to settle in and prepare for what was always a very busy day for him.

As a member of the press, his pass allowed us to park right outside the stadium, which all added to the excitement. We arrived three hours before kick-off but I didn't mind the wait as I tried to take it all in. The atmosphere was electric with fans standing around enjoying each other's company. After what seemed like an eternity we eventually took our seats in the Main Stand but, to our horror, we discovered we were in the middle of the Rangers section! As a nine-year-old, I was blissfully unaware of the situation but I think Mum and Dad were a little uneasy. The game itself was a fantastic affair. The Dons started well but fell behind to a superb John McDonald diving header. All around us Rangers fans celebrated their team taking the lead; we sat quietly and wondered what would happen next. Fortunately we didn't have to wait long as Alex McLeish's superb curling shot ended up in the back of the net. I remember Dad slowly getting to his feet, his hands clenching in fists as the flight of the ball steered towards the top right-hand corner of the net.

He shouted "It's going in" just as the net rippled and we all jumped up in delight but quickly took our seats again as we remembered the company we were keeping. Grunts and groans could be heard from all angles, a deafening moan of discontent but I cared not a jot as my delight was there for all to see. Alex McLeish has spoken of that goal many times and has, on more than one occasion, been quick to quell rumours that the shot was actually a cross!

The Dons played really well in the second half and it was a minor miracle the game went to extra time. In the ensuing thirty minutes, the Dons had too much in their locker for Rangers and ran out very comfortable winners. Mark McGhee headed his side into the lead before Gordon Strachan added a third. We leapt to our feet in joy. As if to make our day complete, Gordon ran in our direction and somersaulted while that little trickle of blood ran out his nose. All that was left was for Neale Cooper to add the final nail in Rangers' coffin when he slammed the ball home into an empty net from a couple of yards. Aberdeen had won the cup for the first time in 12 years!

I have two lasting memories from that game. First, witnessing at close quarters the Rangers fans applauding their team's effort. So many of them stayed behind to offer the players what was a rapturous ovation. As a nine-year-old, I really struggled to understand that mentality as their team had just been humiliated in a major cup final. My other abiding memory was running after Jock Stein in the car park and asking him for his autograph – he duly obliged. He signed my matchday programme and asked if I enjoyed the game? I told him I did and he patted me gently on the head. I still have that programme to this day.

The stuff of dreams

Ask any Aberdeen fan of my generation (born in 1972) what they treasure most from years gone by and I defy anyone not to say the Cup Winners' Cup triumph of the 11th May 1983 against Real Madrid in Gothenburg. The 1982/83 season was the stuff dreams were made of but as a youngster, my mindset was so different. I was used to the Dons winning, it was par for the course and I didn't expect anything less. It was only as I matured and grew older that I truly began to appreciate what a phenomenal feat it really was. The campaign started early...

I was ten-years-old when the Dons welcomed Sion of Switzerland to Pittodrie for a preliminary tie. I can remember, to this day, feeling very excited about going to the stadium as the game was played on a Wednesday night and it was very unusual for my parents to allow me to go to a midweek game. I took my seat in the Merkland Stand with my good friend Angus Fraser and his Mum Betty. We watched in awe as the Dons tore apart the hapless Swiss side, winning 7–0. Angus lived directly behind my house; he wasn't just my friend but our babysitter and football trainer! Angus was a few years older than me but we spent a great deal of time together playing football up on the links near Newburgh beach.

He was an excellent goalkeeper and we spent many a warm solstice evening practising and training. My own game developed thanks to Angus as I would fire shot after shot at him. As he filled the goal and was incredibly agile I knew a cunning plan had to be devised to score be it low down to the corners, a piledriver into the top corner or that area where I believe a goalkeeper struggles the most; smashing shots at a height between hip and knee. It wasn't long before I was taking this new-found strategy into my school games and found scoring goals an almost simple task! Shame this method never materialised into my teens and beyond. Thankfully, being a passionate Aberdeen fan Angus and I found common ground, which continues to this day.

After the Dons smashed Sion into oblivion Angus delivered me safely back to Newburgh where I slept soundly knowing another fine night had just passed. The second leg in the Alps was merely a formality as the Dons ran out very comfortable 4–1 winners. Next up was a little-known team from Albania called Dinamo Tirana. The Albanians gave Aberdeen a torrid time at Pittodrie. I watched the game from the South Stand with Mum and Dad and sat almost in silence as the brand of football on show differed to what I had been used to from our domestic league. The Dinamo players passed the ball on the deck, moved quickly between passes, closed players down, and defended like their lives depended on it.

I was suitably impressed, while at the same time fraught with nerves. Thankfully, after a brilliant move and some magic from Gordon Strachan, John Hewitt was on hand to score the only goal of the game. The second leg was just as difficult but the lads managed to cling on to their 1–0 advantage by playing out a very difficult 0–0 draw. In the next round the Dons faced Lech Poznan from Poland, famous these days for their well-known fan celebration "The Poznan". I always felt confident going into these games as I had never heard of the smaller teams from across Europe so in my own mind they should be a walkover. It's not as if they were AC Milan, Inter, Barcelona or Real Madrid right? I was confident a win would be delivered – it was – 2–0 thanks to two second-half goals from Mark McGhee and Peter Weir.

The second leg was more of a tight affair, which is what you would expect away from Pittodrie. My confidence in the team paid off as a single goal from Mark McGhee was enough to send the Dons into the quarter-finals. Aberdeen fans had to wait a further four months before witnessing the greatest game ever at Pittodrie. When the Dons were drawn against Bayern Munich my instant reaction was one of excitement. I knew of the West German players thanks to the World Cup in Spain the previous summer and looked forward to watching these superstars in the flesh. Managed by the great Uli Hoeness, the German giants had a team full of internationals, Paul Breitner, Karl-Heinz Rummenigge and Klaus Augenthaler to name but a few. It would take a massive effort from the Dons but being young and naïve, losing never entered my youthful mind.

With the first leg not shown live on TV, we spent Wednesday evening listening to the game on the radio. I really hoped we could get something from the match as days before Franz Beckenbauer had upset me with comments he made in the paper in regards to Aberdeen's inferior technical abilities. I took an instant dislike to "Der Kaiser". That night the Dons shoved those words right down Mr Beckenbauer's throat as the performance was one of the finest witnessed by any Scottish team on foreign shores. The Dons secured a very credible 0–0 draw but could, and maybe should, have won the match.

The 16th March 1983 is one of the fondest days of my life as an Aberdeen fan. I was still a relatively new kid on the block but for two years the Dons had become a massive part of my life. After this match my passion for the team reached new heights. That day at school I could not concentrate, I was so excited. During break-time, the boys and I played out what we believed would happen that night at Pittodrie. I always played Willie Miller, running around the small park at the back of the school like a kid possessed. I had so much energy I didn't want our short breaks to end.

I walked home with a spring in my step knowing it was only a matter of dinner, bath and then into the car for the drive up to the beach. It was a clear evening across the city that night but the chill in the air was very much in evidence as we made the short walk across the golf links to the stadium. Dad secured our seats in the Main Stand just above the players' tunnel. I was happy to sit there but a pillar obstructed the Merkland Stand goal. "You have got to be joking," I cheekily said to Dad. "Just be grateful you're here," he quickly retorted. I squirmed back into my seat, took another bite of my sausage roll and waited impatiently for the game to kick off.

As we arrived a good 30 minutes before the match commenced I was able to see at close-quarters the lads running out and returning from the tunnel before and after their pre-match warm-up. I stood and watched with a huge grin on my face as the players trotted back into the dressing room, stopping to sign the odd autograph on the way in. I kept turning round to Mum and saying; "Look, there's Mark McGhee, Mum; look there's Peter Weir; Mum, look, there's Gordon Strachan." She always replied with "yes, darling, I can see them". As both sets of players made their way onto the park for the game, they were met with a noise I doubt I will ever hear again at Pittodrie. All around fans were on their feet clapping, cheering and a deafening chorus of "come on you reds" reverberated around the stadium; the atmosphere was incredible.

At last we were ready for kick-off. The side Alex Ferguson picked was arguably the best he could have possibly selected. The Germans started strongly and it was no surprise when they took the lead. Bayern's talisman at the back, Klaus Augenthaler, smashed the ball high into the net from 25 yards. I had seen the German international do this before on TV and as soon as he picked the ball up and made room for himself I knew it was going in. I looked at my Dad for some reasoning but he just looked at me and shrugged his shoulders. All around us it was quiet for the first time since we took our seats.

The Dons looked out of it for long parts of the game but, as I fully hoped and expected, found a path back into the match when Neil Simpson smashed the ball home after some good work by Gordon Strachan and Mark McGhee in the build-up. My Dad was on his feet instantly punching the air; he looked down at me and offered me a huge grin. I simply jumped up and down and waved my scarf high above my head. For long periods, Pittodrie had been quiet but Simmie's goal gave the fans a lift and the atmosphere soon returned. "Stand free" and "come on you reds" bellowed out across the night sky.

In 1983, I still had no understanding of the away goal; in fact I doubt I actually knew it existed in European games. So, as we stood in the queue for our half-time refreshment, Dad explained that Aberdeen needed to score another as Bayern actually led the tie on the away goals rule. I still felt confident we could do it! The next 45 minutes was like nothing I had ever experienced before. At a young age, emotions are still very much in the development stage but that cold night I clearly remember feeling the type of excitement and trepidation that you can only sample at football matches. It was an emotional rollercoaster with 24,999 others on board. Aberdeen started the second half brightly but then the unimaginable happened. Bayern scored again! As Hans Pfugler connected with his volley, I clearly remember Dad saying, "It's going in". Pittodrie fell quiet as the enormity of the task in hand was staring us all in the face. At 2–1 down I, for one, thought it was all over.

I asked Dad what Aberdeen needed to do but he stared into space; Mum put her arm around me. What happened from there on in is nothing like I've ever experienced before, or likely to again. Fergie made a change, bringing on John Hewitt for the closing stages of the game. I don't know what was said to John by Fergie but out of nothing the game was turned on its head.

First, the free kick that fooled everybody, a moment of pure genius from Gordon Strachan and John McMaster as everyone in the stadium gave out a huge sigh when both pretended to confuse each other. I couldn't believe it but within the blink of an eye the ball was delivered into the box and big Alex McLeish headed home the equaliser. We all jumped to our feet, arms high in the air, I grabbed Dad's arm as I cheered a brilliantly worked goal; Mum and Dad were clapping wildly; Dad screaming "come on Dons". I joined in, the excitement in me boiling over. Pittodrie came alive again. Fans on their feet, grown men screaming at the top of their voices, women covering their mouths with their hands wondering, just wondering if only! I swear in that moment I felt Pittodrie move!

Then the moment that will never be forgotten by those present that night. Almost as soon as I had taken my seat after the celebrations I looked up and saw the ball being delivered into the box. As Dad and the folk around us slowly came off their seats, Eric Black got his head to the ball. As Dad came up a little higher, he headed towards goal. Dad sat up a little higher still, fists clenched, jaws agape, I couldn't see what was happening; he was in front of me as was that great big iron pillar! As I tried to push my way through, Bayern's goalkeeper palmed the ball down, a gasp rose from the crowd, John Hewitt was there, he connected and then bedlam!! All around us people were going berserk, the players were running towards the 18-yard box, Dad was jumping up and down; Mum was cheering and clapping like a woman demented.

Had we scored again? I shouted to Dad, grabbing him; "What's happened?" I screamed. He looked down at me, "They've scored again, kiddo, they've scored again." I must confess to feeling a bit lost at that point. I didn't understand what had happened. Did we need to score again because of the away goal? "Dad, Dad," I shouted, "do we need another goal?" "No," he roared back, "we're winning 3–2, we're winning." I couldn't believe it. We had turned the game on its head and were heading towards the semi-finals. At that moment Pittodrie did move, the whole place lifted by 25,000 fans jumping up and down, hugging, crying, and my God what a moment!

The closing minutes of that game were almost unbearable. It seemed like an age before the referee finally blew his whistle to bring the game to an end. The full-time whistle was met with jubilation. It was a fantastic moment as I watched the lads celebrate on the pitch with the back-room staff. Pittodrie was electric. As the team made their way off the park, I stood on my seat with Mum holding me tight, cheering, clapping and singing. We stayed behind for some minutes as we enjoyed the atmosphere, then the team re-appeared. It was brilliant, a lap of honour and quite rightly so. What an achievement and what a game. I didn't want to leave Pittodrie that night!

For two days I was on cloud nine until the very next game at Pittodrie when all came crashing down around us as the boys lost 2–1 to Dundee United. I couldn't understand why we lost that game, how we could beat one of Europe's greatest but yet play so badly against United; it didn't make sense. I was confused, upset and annoyed. Dad explained to me that fatigue had probably set in and the efforts of the previous Wednesday had taken its toll on the team but I didn't accept his reasons for the defeat. I was angry, I felt betrayed and sulked for the rest of the weekend!

My misery was compounded a few days later as the draw for the semi-final pitted the Dons against little-known Belgian side Waterschei. Dad was unable to get us tickets for the game despite promises to the contrary. It proved to be the only home game we missed in the whole campaign. Pittodrie could have been sold out twice due to the huge demand. I was on the verge of tears when Dad told me; my world came crashing down. We had followed the boys through thick and thin from the first game against Sion to the epic against Bayern Munich; I had kicked every ball, made every tackle, cheered and shouted until my throat was hoarse. Now, here was the semi-final of a major European competition, arguably the biggest game in the club's history and I couldn't be part of it; I was distraught.

The night of the game I decided I would go out and play football with my mates, as I didn't want to listen to the game on the radio. I'd made my mind up if I couldn't be part of it, I didn't want anything to do with it. I know the ignorance of youth played a major role in my decision but I wish I had paid attention to both Mum and Dad when they told me to take my seat at the kitchen table and listen to the game on the radio. I was not for swaying and out I went searching for my friends to have a kick-about.

However, my inquisitiveness got the better of me and it wasn't long before I was back home finding out the score. When Dad shouted through the front window that the Dons were 2–0 up a huge grin appeared across my face and all my anger dissipated. I knew the highlights were on TV so I came back in from playing football early, grabbed a bath, made sure my homework was up to speed and asked politely if I could stay up to watch. I couldn't wait for the game to come on TV, having already learned the result I knew this was going to be special, and so it proved as the Dons completely outclassed the Belgians.

I expected us to win but never a 5–1 thumping. Dougie Bell was immense; Neil Simpson's goal was outstanding, a truly brilliant display. Surely we had one foot in the final? I suppose the only blot on the landscape for the Dons was the 0–1 reverse in Belgium; our only defeat of the campaign but, thankfully, the job had already been done. Aberdeen were through to their first European final. That very same night I begged and pleaded with Dad to take us to Gothenburg to watch the Dons against the mighty Real Madrid. The nagging continued for days but my Dad was rock steady in his usual reply, "we'll see". Little did I know the cunning plan he had already conceived for the game, a masterstroke from my Dad for which I will always be grateful.

Gothenburg

The Dons had to wait just over three weeks for the Cup Winners' Cup Final against Real Madrid. The city was buzzing. I was buzzing, but had no concrete answer from Dad until one sunny evening exactly seven days before the match. Dad arrived home from work. I went over to greet him and he gave me his usual hug and asked how my day had been. Without the blink of an eye but wearing a cheeky smirk on his face, he asked me if I would like to go to Gothenburg for the final. I couldn't quite believe my ears; it took a couple of seconds for it to sink in. I screamed, "Yes, yes of course". I grabbed him and held him tight. He then asked me if I would like my best friend Ewan Taylor to come with us.

This was too much, my best friend as well, no way!! I was delirious with happiness. Ewan and I had been friends from the off. Our families moved to the village within months of each other and a strong bond grew from day one, which I'm delighted to say has lasted the course. I was thrilled to attend his wedding to the lovely Nicky and was overjoyed when his dad Willie bag-piped my own wife Miriam into church on our wedding day.

After Dad told me the unbelievable news, I told him I would be back in a bit and ran round to Ewan's house and walked straight in without knocking and ran up to his room where he was doing his homework. I almost yelled at him that we were going to Gothenburg; his face was a picture! I was overcome with excitement; I ran back downstairs, apologised to Mr and Mrs Taylor for my abrupt entrance, and ran all the way home to find out more from Dad about our trip.

Over dinner he explained he was organising a host of flights from Aberdeen Airport to Gothenburg for the fans. Our neighbour Joe was in attendance, as was our local bank manager Billy Bremner (Dad knew how to keep the important people sweet). It was going to be brilliant. I must admit I felt sorry for my younger brother Peter; I wanted him to come with us but back in May 1983 Peter was still only seven-years-old and too young to make the trip so he had to be content with staying with friends for the night and watching the game on TV. To make up for him missing out and to ease my lasting guilt I arranged many years later for the members of that successful team to autograph a replica Cup Winners' Cup shirt that I presented to him for his 30th birthday. That very shirt takes pride of place in his bedroom alongside pictures of his two gorgeous children, Poppy and Emma.

In 1983 Dad worked for a small aviation company called Peregrine Airlines, which operated out of Aberdeen Airport. With the help of others, he organised through his own company "Grampian Air Charter" special flights back and forth to Sweden. Each flight was packed full of expectant fans. We left the morning of the match – early! I was so excited I could hardly contain myself. Ewan and I donned our tops and dressed from head to toe in red and white. The airport was jammed full of Aberdeen fans heading for Gothenburg, with camera crews, photographers and press people running about looking for the perfect anecdote for their respective newspapers, radio and TV stations. It was like a circus had just landed at Aberdeen Airport.

The mood was high; from all angles Dons fans were singing, laughing, joking, and drinking!! It was brilliant and I did my best to try and take it all in. As soon as we took off and levelled out, Dad whipped out his old camera and started recording the fans on the plane (this footage was used by BBC Alba in their special 30th anniversary documentary). Everybody was so jovial. Ewan and I instantly fell asleep due to the early start! I missed the entire flight and had to be woken by Mum as we prepared for our final descent into Gothenburg Airport. Upon our arrival, I clearly remember the dull weather. It didn't feel like we were in a foreign country!

Had we actually made it to Sweden? Then it dawned on me as the penny dropped, all around me the womenfolk were blonde... and gorgeous! I fell in love instantly and my affection for blondes has remained to this day! That was my first impression of Sweden; the next was the futuristic bus Dad organised to transport us to our hotel. It was ever so fabulous and high tech; it even had TVs. It was amazing! Reclining leather seats with cup holders; I thought I had died and gone to heaven! The atmosphere in Gothenburg city centre was electric. Everywhere we ventured Dons fans were very much in evidence. I remember, in particular, a small shopping arcade, which appeared to be taken over by the Red Army. I genuinely believe the locals enjoyed our company just as much as we enjoyed theirs. Spirits were high and the mood was one of excitement. It was a testimony to all Aberdeen fans on the trip that not a single arrest was made. As we ate lunch in one of the many café bars it started to rain. Nothing unusual about this, but the rain continued late into the afternoon and then into the evening, becoming heavier and heavier.

As we made our way back to the hotel to get ready for the game the rain became torrential. The adult folk started to express some concerns about the possibility of the game being cancelled. To be honest, at this point I was unperturbed and very much looking forward to making our way to the stadium.

Mum made sure Ewan and I were adequately wrapped up, safe from the elements. At last we were on our way! As we made our way to the stadium on our luxury bus, I looked out through the steamy windows to the skyline and wondered if it would ever stop raining. We passed taxis full of Aberdeen fans, minibuses with flags and scarves flapping in the wind. My excitement grew and grew as we edged ever closer.

Dad told Ewan and I to look directly ahead and there, for the first time, I caught a glimpse of the Ullevi Stadium; it was magnificent and the floodlights were the biggest I had ever seen. The steel structure that dominated my view was just as spectacular as I hoped it would be. The driver dropped us right outside the main entrance. As we stepped off the bus, the rain continued to lash down soaking us to the skin. Billy had the ingenious idea of buying some rain macs but little did we know at the time how ridiculous we must have all looked sporting the garish yellow macs which covered us from head to toe.

Ewan and I looked as though we had been swamped in a small marquee! However, as ridiculous as we may have looked, they certainly did the job and kept the rain at bay. We made our way into the stadium, passed security and up the small steel staircase to the terracing. I remember looking out at the pitch and it looked drenched; the night sky was dark and grey and my face was stinging from the lashing rain. Dad led us to a spot which he thought was a good vantage point but I couldn't see anything apart from some guy's arse in my face so I pleaded with him to move us. He decided, with the blessing of all, to move further down towards the bottom of the terracing.

There was no point looking for cover as, by this point, we were all soaked to the skin so we might as well try and get a decent spot where we all can watch the match without obstruction. We made our way further down towards the perimeter fence where the view was fantastic; I could see everything, even the far goal looked clear. Let the game commence! We arrived in the stadium just as the teams were coming out. The noise was deafening, even over the pouring rain. For the first time I looked up behind me and realised just how many fans had made the trip; it was an awe-inspiring sight as the second tier was awash with banners, flags, and thousands of waving scarves. I stood and watched this sea of red and white for a good few minutes; the image is still ingrained in my memory today.

I then looked over to my far left to catch a glimpse of the Real Madrid fans and was left disappointed as hardly any had bothered to make the trip to follow their team. I asked Dad why this was so and he said maybe it was down to the fact it was Aberdeen they were playing in the final and didn't see the need to travel as the Spanish fully expected to win without even breaking sweat. This confused me and I took an instant dislike to them, especially the annoying drummer Manuel who I remembered from the World Cup! Kick-off was met with another roar from the Red Army and off we went. Ewan and I huddled close to each other; I suppose I was looking for some comfort as my nerves were getting the better of me.

The Dons started strongly and before I had time to settle after the excitement of kick-off, a long ball was delivered to the edge of the 18-yard box where Eric Black majestically swivelled and hit a stunning scissor-kick volley which smashed off the bar. We all held our heads in our hands and looked at each other in disbelief. What a brilliant start! As the first half progressed, Aberdeen were more than holding their own against the mighty Real and it wasn't long before our dreams became reality. From a cleverly-worked Gordon Strachan corner, Alex McLeish made a late run to the edge of the 18-yard box and connected firmly with a header which he directed goalwards. The ball hit a Real defender and fell to the feet of Eric Black who instinctively turned and fired a shot past the diving Agustin.

All around us Aberdeen fans were cheering wildly and celebrating the opening goal. In that moment it felt like the rain had stopped and sunny clouds appeared over the Ullevi Stadium. The game wasn't even a quarter old when our joy turned to despair. Real equalised! The pitch was heavy and bogged down with excess water. It did not make for a great spectacle but it was obvious from watching the game on DVD years later that the Spanish giants had the better of the first half. I always find it interesting how, as a youngster, my take on the game completely differs from that as an adult.

When the club released the 25th anniversary DVD of the game, I was pleasantly surprised to see how well the Dons actually played. It was going on many years since I last saw the game and memories of events obviously faded with time. But I certainly have not forgotten the back-pass from Alex McLeish which held up on the sodden pitch. Our vantage point meant we had the perfect view of the ball sticking and Real's forward Santillana seizing the opportunity. As he shifted the ball past Jim Leighton, Jim brought Real's captain tumbling to the floor. No doubt – a penalty! I stood and gazed for a second, trying to understand what had just happened. Alex stood with his hands on his head and a deathly silence fell over the Dons fans. Juanito stepped up and sent Jim the wrong way, 1–1! SHIT! Or words of a similar effect a ten-year-old would say!

For the first time since arriving at the stadium, I sat down on the sodden benches. Ewan joined me and we tried to convince ourselves everything would be OK. The Spaniards dominated up until half-time without really looking like adding to the score-line. At the interval, the menfolk disappeared to try and find us something warm to drink as the cold was starting to set in. The rain continued to fall heavily and I was starting to feel a little miserable. Mum did her best to lift our spirits and told us to keep cheering the Dons on, which would help keep us warm. The small cup of tea that Dad brought me went down a treat! The second half kicked off and it was Fergie's qualities as a manager that really shone through as the Dons took control with Gordon Strachan, Doug Rougvie, John McMaster and Peter Weir shining. Real offered little as the conditions sapped their energy but yet the Dons still couldn't make the breakthrough.

Dad explained to Ewan and I that extra time might have to be played, then penalties if need be. The extra time didn't bother me but penalties we could well do without! Once the referee blew the full-time whistle, the Dons fans lifted the place again with more songs and kept the atmosphere going. I've always wondered if the fans' enthusiasm that night rubbed off on the players as Fergie and co gave their instructions for the ensuing half-an-hour's extra play. So off we went again. It was a gruelling period for both teams but Aberdeen appeared to have that little bit more in their tank, their stamina a testimony to their fitness levels. By contrast, Real seemed to find it difficult to cope. The Dons carved out a few chances, notably a header from Eric Black which he put over when it appeared easier to score. Peter Weir was sen-sational. Weir danced his way past defenders, bamboozling them with his array of skills and runs and ultimately contrib-uting to the most magical moment in Dons history. Gordon Strachan had a volley superbly saved by Agustin. If it had been placed either side of the Real goalkeeper I'm sure the ball would have nestled in the back of the net and the course of history would have changed. But maybe fate played a huge part that night for one young player, John Hewitt.

Hewitt replaced Eric Black who had run himself into the ground. There was a sense of anticipation among the Dons fans when John came on, could history repeat itself? He had done it once so famously against Bayern Munich, could he go one step further and do it against the mighty Real? As the clock ticked down, Aberdeen broke up a Real move; Peter Weir picked the ball up on the left wing and beat a couple of players. I can clearly remember Mark McGhee taking up the outside-left position as Peter floated a ball into his path. Mark made for the byline. John Hewitt at this point was gently jogging his way towards the edge of the box; all around us people sensed something was going to happen. I was off my seat, now standing on the bench for a better look.

Mark dragged the ball past a defender with his right foot, in turn creating space for a cross. Hewitt made a dash for the penalty spot, anticipating where the ball could fall. McGhee pinged the ball over with his left foot, Agustin dived but missed, I saw Hewitt dive, connect, then... pandemonium!! The ball hit the back of the net. A noise like nothing I'd ever heard hit my ears. My Dad jumped for joy, as did all the adults in the travelling party. Ewan threw his arms in the air! But, at this very same point in time, the one moment revered by all connected with the club has fallen from my memory. All my recollections of how I personally celebrated have evaporated; I can't remember how I reacted!!!

I remember Hewitt's comical star jump, Doug Rougvie running the length of the pitch to celebrate with him. Did I cheer, did I go mad like so many around me, and did I jump up and down? I honestly can't remember and I'm devastated. I can recall so much from my childhood but the one moment which I want to cherish has gone! I had to rely on the memories of Mum and Dad and they ensured me that I went ballistic. According to my Mum, I made my way with Ewan towards the perimeter fence to get closer to Hewitt and Rougvie. She told me I did a comical dance and she tried to hold me back as she didn't want to lose sight of me. Apparently, all the adults watched on in amusement as Ewan and I with arms on each other's shoulders jumped up and down in glee. It was a truly fantastic moment, one that will never be experienced again in my lifetime.

The closing minutes of the game clawed at my nerves. What was only eight minutes felt like eight hours! Then, without warning, Real were awarded a free kick just outside the 18-yard box. It was horrible. I didn't want to watch. I held my breath as Salguero fired in a low drive; I thought it was going in but at the last moment it flew past the post. A huge cheer went up and Dad shouted "come on ref, blow the whistle!!" I looked at him and he smiled, a smile that was the reassurance I needed that the game was over. Leighton kicked off and that was that, the ref blew for full time and the whole place erupted. We stood with arms in the air, hugging each other, laughing, some around us were crying, what a moment! It had even stopped raining!

The players and coaching staff spilled onto the pitch and the celebrations began. It was an awe-inspiring scene to watch these guys share history in the making. The Real players looked on in shock but I didn't care about them. As Willie Miller received the trophy and held it aloft in that now iconic pose, a huge roar went up. We cheered every player who stood and held the trophy high into the Gothenburg sky. The lap of honour quickly followed and the rain that had fallen so heavily was now replaced with scarves, flags and hats raining down on the pitch. For me time stood still. I didn't want it to end. I wanted the players to stay out on the pitch forever. I wanted to stay rooted to the spot for all time but I knew at some point we would have to leave. After the players made their way back into the dressing room, the travelling support slowly started to break up and head out into the streets, where the party began. All around us fans were singing, dancing and congratulating each other on a magnificent achievement. Spirits were at an all-time high. As we made our way to the bus an incident occurred that no doubt will stay with me till the day I die.

Out the corner of my eye I noticed a taxi pull up and the passenger door swing open. A figure fell out and I couldn't help but look and smile at this uncouth character as he fell out the cab and into a large puddle on the street. At the same time as he hit the deck, his legs came up behind him. His kilt flew over the top of his head exposing him in all his glory for all to see. His bagpipes quickly followed out the cab offering a whine as they came to rest. Mum grabbed both Ewan and I and tried to cover our eyes, almost as if she was frightened Ewan and I would be scarred for life. It was hilarious; the menfolk lifted this poor chap to his feet and asked him if he was OK? In a drunken slur he said "aye" and proceeded to ask Dad what time kick-off was? We all stopped in our tracks, not quite comprehending what the man had just asked.

Dad told him he had missed the game, that it finished nearly an hour ago and that the Dons had won 2–1. It took a few seconds for this information to register with the poor chap and once the penny dropped the realisation of his actions meant a rapid sobering up! I was shocked; I couldn't quite believe he had missed the game, not just any game but the biggest game in the club's history. Leaving the guy to sober up, we all boarded our bus and talked about the game all the way back to the hotel. Once inside the warmth of our room, we relaxed and chilled out as we had to catch our flight back to Aberdeen at some ungodly hour. Mum wanted Ewan and I to sleep but the adrenaline was still pumping through our bodies so she allowed us to stay up and play board games until the time came to get back on the bus and make our way to the airport. The airport was almost deserted but for a few fans milling about waiting for their flights. Ewan and I loved the vast empty spaces of the airport; it was like a huge playground.

Dad bought us a small ball so we played football in the terminal and re-enacted the moment John Hewitt scored the winner. A couple of older guys approached us and asked if they could join in, so one hour before we flew back to Aberdeen – 4am local time – a bunch of rowdy Aberdeen fans had a wee game of football in the departure lounge of Gothenburg Airport! I don't have any recollections of the flight home as once aboard the exhaustion hit me like a train and I was out for the count before we took off. The next thing I knew we were landing at Dyce Airport. While waiting for the bags, Dad bought all the morning newspapers. One story dominated not just the front pages but the back too: Aberdeen beating the mighty Real Madrid to lift the Cup Winners' Cup. Sitting on the floor, reading the *P&J*, Dad suggested we go to Pittodrie to welcome the boys home. My first thought was school as Ewan and I were both due back that morning but unbeknown to us Mum had already organised for us to have the day off! Now this was just too much, not only had I been to Gothenburg to watch Aberdeen in their finest hour but also

I'm now getting an extra day off school!

We made our way back to Newburgh from the airport and I couldn't wait to get home. I was looking forward to reading more of the papers, watching the reports on TV and getting ready to go to Pittodrie. We dropped everybody off one by one, said our goodbyes and then we were home! What a trip it had been; I was still very tired but buzzing. After freshening up, we were all ready to make our way to Pittodrie to welcome home the boys. We quickly drove round to the primary school where Mum had pre-arranged for Peter to be picked up so he could come with us. As we waited outside for Peter to appear, some of my classmates and friends gathered round for a glimpse of the two boys who had just been to Gothenburg seated tightly together in the back of Dad's car. Ewan and I felt like celebrities and we offered a wave and a smile back!

Once at Pittodrie, we were met with a sea of red and white and I was amazed how many were in the stadium considering it was a Thursday afternoon. After what felt like an eternity, the team eventually appeared from the players' tunnel to a standing ovation and rapturous applause. We watched on from the main stand as the players slowly made their way round the perimeter of the pitch with camera crews, reporters and photographers in tow. Some fans had spilled onto the pitch, which added to the atmosphere, all clambering for a closer look at the Cup Winners' Cup but it was all in good humour and nobody stepped out of line. We stood on the old wooden seats and clapped wildly as the team passed us by, waving at each individual player. I'm convinced they all saw me and gave me a personal wave back; well, I would like to think so anyway! We must have spent two or three hours inside the stadium but it was worth it as the welcome the team received was on a par with the game itself. It took me days to come down from the whole experience; some memories have faded but most have remained and I feel privileged and fortunate to have been one of the 18,000 to have made the trip to Sweden.

Europe's finest

More success followed in December when the Dons were officially crowned the best team in Europe after beating SV Hamburg over two legs. In the days leading up to the first leg in Germany, I was aware of the important game but naïve to the level of significance. For me it was just another match. As it was not covered on TV like so many other midweek nights, I lay in bed listening on the radio. I fell asleep before full time and rushed downstairs the very next morning to grab the paper before anyone else could lay their hands on it. The headline greeted me kindly, 0–0. Great result, even though I felt a little disappointed a win was not delivered. As I read the match report it was obvious the Dons had been unlucky not to come away with a victory. Mark McGhee, in particular, was guilty of wasting a great chance when he danced his way past numerous Hamburg defenders inside the 18-yard box only to smash a low drive off the goalkeeper's legs. Like so many other mornings during my primary school days I walked to school with a spring in my step.

Thankfully, I only had to wait one week before the return leg at Pittodrie. I begged Dad for tickets and like so many times before, he delivered. He didn't need much persuasion to stand outside the ticket office in the driving wind and rain. The night of the game, the 20th December 1983, was a cold, damp, miserable evening. There was a chill in the Pittodrie air but the atmosphere soon made up for it. Dad took the unusual step of buying tickets further down the Main Stand nearer the pitch. In fact, we were directly halfway down with a great view towards the Merkland Road goal. No metal stanchion obstruction made for an even happier 11-year-old fan, wrapped up tightly, and tucking into a newly purchased sausage roll, a sneaky treat by one's father!

The first half went by in a flash, a tight affair with both sides cancelling each other out. Dad and I jumped up and down to keep warm during the break, Dad telling me to clap my hands together to keep them warm. I was starting to feel the cold as the players made their way out for the second period. Thankfully, within moments of the re-start, I was warm again. The Dons swept into first gear and delivered the sucker punch. I watched carefully as Peter Weir made one of his dazzling runs down the wing, delivered a superb ball across the 18-yard box, John Hewitt didn't quite connect but the ball fell beautifully to Neil Simpson who smashed it home from 12 yards. Cue wild celebrations as Pittodrie once again went berserk. I was jumping up and down with my arms in the air as Dad cheered on. He looked down at me and winked as he always did in these situations.

I knew there and then the Dons would go on and win the Super Cup. Not long after the singing had died down it reached new levels as the Dons took an unassailable two-goal lead. From a Peter Weir corner right in front of us, Willie Miller got the slightest of touches and Mark McGhee was on hand to drill the ball home. I jumped up out of my seat, even before the ball hit the back of the net. I knew instinctively after Willie's touch it was going to be another goal. As I stood cheering, Dad was standing punching the air, shouting at the top of his voice "yes, yes". I stood and watched on in astonishment. Here was my Dad who in usual circumstances was fairly conservative in his celebration, but not tonight. He was screaming at the top of his voice, punching the night air.

I told you earlier in the book my experience with Dad when Archie Gemmill scored for Scotland against Holland; here I was again but this time older and with a better understanding of the game. I allowed myself to put my own celebrations on hold to observe him. I closed my eyes and remembered the moment sitting on my Mum's knee watching him jump up and down as a five-year-old. I gently reminisced as Pittodrie once again erupted, a calming moment when all around me was in bedlam. That moment has never left my mind; I can still see him today punching his wrists through the air. I can still hear him shouting, eyes popping out his head.

For years afterwards I always wondered if he would replicate such an act, but he never did. He celebrated many more triumphs with the family but his celebrations remained traditional. Even when I played schoolboy football and scored, he remained calm and applauded politely. The only other time he allowed himself to get a little over-excited was when I scored my boys' club third and decisive goal in the final of the Aberdeen International Football Festival in the summer of 1987. As I headed home in front of nearly 3,000 people at Seaton Park, I managed to pick both him and Mum out in the crowd. As I caught his eye I could see the delight etched across his face. I had only seen this before in Gothenburg, and that night at Pittodrie five days before Christmas in 1983.

The Super Cup now hangs in the boardroom at Pittodrie. It's a small wooden number with the golden Uefa crest dominating the centre of the plaque. I've been extremely fortunate to get up close and personal with the now famous artefact and it's a timely reminder of a memorable night spent with my Dad celebrating yet another fine win.

Season 1982/83 will go down in the annals of the club's history as the greatest ever. Being relatively young in both age, and as a fan, some memories have faded but the whole season from beginning to end was a fantastic ride. After attending the 1982 Scottish Cup Final, I expected the Dons to carry on where they left off. It was a privilege to watch, at first hand, their incredible achievements. The Dons reached the final the following year but the path was fraught with difficult games, with only one home tie throughout the entire campaign. My first trip to Easter Road in Edinburgh for the third round proved to be as memorable with the side brushing aside Hibs 4–1. I was really looking forward to watching the match as it was the first time I had seen Scotland's keeper Alan Rough in the flesh. All my preconceptions of the man were not to be denied, he was shocking!

For the quarter-finals we happened to be in Glasgow for a family gathering so it was the perfect excuse to ask my grandpa to take me to Firhill to watch the lads against Partick Thistle. It just so happened he was also working so I watched the game from the old press box high in the Main Stand. Grandpa introduced me to a certain gentleman called Ally MacLeod. I said "hello" quietly while keeping close to my grandpa's side. I had no idea the man shaking my hand was the former Aberdeen and Scotland manager! The innocence of youth very much in evidence!

For the semi-final Aberdeen were due to play Celtic at Hampden and when I asked Dad if we could go, I received the usual "we'll see" but I knew deep down he fancied it. I was proved right only a few days later when it was confirmed grandpa had secured four tickets. As always we drove down on the Friday night after school and stayed in Bishopbriggs. I loved the drive down; it was always filled with excitement. Peter and I hung our scarves out the back windows and a huge flag was draped across the back ledge of the car.

Thinking back, this was a rather pointless exercise as it was dark outside!

The morning of the game I went through my usual routine, reading the papers, watching a spot of TV and having a kick-about with Peter in the back garden. Soon we were ready for the off. Arriving at Hampden early we had an opportunity to see the team bus arrive. I begged Dad to take me over so I could get a good look at the lads emerging, dressed in their smart club blazers, and looking very much the heroes that they were. Peter and I were thrilled. The game itself was not for the faint-hearted as the physical battle determined the pattern of play. Neale Cooper broke his nose, Dougie Bell, Eric Black and Gordon Strachan all received knocks. Thankfully, that did not deter the spirit which was very much in evidence as the Dons found an extra gear and won 1–0 thanks to a Peter Weir header at the back post. Weir had come on as a second-half substitute and turned the game on its head. (Forgive the pun.)

The goal was met with elation from the Aberdeen section away to our left; I stood and watched in awe at the sea of red and white celebrating another vital goal. It was enough to send the Dons through to their second successive Scottish Cup Final. The 1983 Scottish Cup Final itself will always be remembered as something of an anti-climax to a wonderful week. But, in the days leading up to the game, it was all go. It was a marvellous few days, arriving back from Gothenburg in the early hours of the Thursday morning, bunking off school to watch the side arrive back at Pittodrie and then another trip to Glasgow for yet another final. It was an incredibly exciting period but I sensed exhaustion on the part of Mum and Dad. It really was non-stop but I clearly recall loving every minute of it. Once again we were positioned among the

Rangers fans in the far left-hand corner of the Main Stand.

The game itself was a huge anti-climax. The Aberdeen players certainly didn't do themselves justice with the performance that day but yet again they dug deep and Eric Black scored what proved to be the winner four minutes from the end of extra time. Like the many thousands of fans who made the trip from the north-east we stayed on to watch the lap of honour and applaud the lads' achievements. As the players made their way past the Main Stand the celebrations appeared to be slightly muted; there wasn't the normal spring in the step or jovial banter between the lads. It was my Dad that noticed it first; he offered exhaustion as an excuse. It was many years later I learned that Fergie had ripped into the team in a post-match TV interview, calling the performance "disgraceful". I'm sure he regretted those comments but it just goes to show the standards Alex Ferguson set. I understand the players upon learning of the said comments were not exactly overjoyed having performed minor miracles to win the Cup Winners' Cup only days earlier. I believe Alex Ferguson had every right to have a go at the team's performance that day. It was another day – another game and they allowed their high standards to slip. Alex Ferguson reminded them very publicly that those standards had now been set and he expected the players to follow suit. I know it's an old saying but if you can't stand the heat and all that! If there was ever proof of Alex Ferguson's standards it was there for all to see in that TV interview. Oh, and let's not forget the small matter of the Dons just becoming the first club outside the Old Firm to retain the famous old trophy! Just thought I would throw that one in!

Out of pocket

As winners of the Cup Winners' Cup, Aberdeen automatically qualified for the following campaign as holders of the trophy, although they would have qualified anyway as Scottish Cup winners. The competition offered so much but, ultimately, ended in defeat, and more importantly for my family, there were financial implications to boot. I would only learn about this many years later. The competition started in mid-September 1983 against little-known Icelandic side IA Akranes. The job was done in the first leg with a 2–1 win, although a sloppy performance in the second at Pittodrie was not exactly welcomed by us the fans! Next up was Belgian Cup winners Beveren, with the first match away. That first leg finished 0–0 and I knew there and then we would have too much for them at Pittodrie. Ahead of the game the Dons were boosted by the news manager Alex Ferguson had just signed a new five-year deal which made him the highest paid manager in Scotland...and rightly so! The ovation he received as he made his way to the dugout that evening was the perfect boost ahead of kick-off.

The Dons were nothing short of brilliant and tore the Beveren defence apart. Gordon Strachan, in particular, orchestrated everything from midfield and ran the show. Even with a nose injury nothing could stop him from having another outstanding game. The Merkland Stand choir were in fine voice throughout as we joined in the songs from beginning to end. I can't help but think that Alex Ferguson's commitment to the club rubbed off on both the players and fans, as the

Pittodrie atmosphere was electric. Once again the quarter-finals beckoned and this time the Dons were paired with Ujpest Dozsa from Hungary. No problem, I thought, as the draw was made. Those words would come back to haunt me. I asked Mum if I could stay up to listen to the game on the radio but as it was a school night a swift "no" was delivered. I took no particular pleasure in going to bed when I knew the Dons were playing, as I tossed and turned wondering how the lads were getting on; going to bed seemed to defeat the purpose of sleep.

As soon as I woke from my slumber the next morning, I was downstairs like a flash, grabbing the newspaper from the porch and quickly reading the headline on the back page. I was not ready for what was staring back at me in black and white print. The Dons had been beaten 2–0! I couldn't believe it. Was it a misprint? Should it not have read the other way round? Surely it was the Dons who had won 2–0? But no, as I read the report it dawned on me the Dons had in fact lost a game they should have won, and won comfortably. I went to school that morning very upset. The return leg at Pittodrie would be another memorable night. Never in the club's history had the Dons overcome a two-goal deficit in a European game but Mark McGhee would re-write that particular passage in the history books. Pittodrie was packed to the rafters with an atmosphere on par with the Munich game. As was my will in those days my powers of persuasion got the better of Mum and Dad and both relented without any fuss and decided a trip to Pittodrie was a must for what could be another momentous night.

We took our seats in the South Stand on a relatively cold evening towards the end of March. I was nervous and wondered how the Dons would cope. To calm my nerves, I sat quietly and read the matchday programme. I read Fergie's notes, taking in all the words, looking for inspiration. As I turned to the letters page imagine my shock when staring back at me was my Dad's own name! There in front of me was a poem penned by my own Dad! It took me a moment to comprehend what I was reading, my Dad, in *The Don*!! I grabbed him by the arm and said "look, look, you're in the programme". He looked down, smiled at me and said "ah yes, your Dad is a man of many talents", which made me laugh. He told me he had written the poem months before and sent it to the club to see if they would print it which, of course, they did! It all added to the incredible excitement that night. Below is a copy of my Dad's poem:

We went across to Gothie
My neighbour Joe and me
We went to see the Dons play
Not watch it on TV.

The Dons had reached the final
Of a European cup
They needed lots of lads like us
To cheer and whip them up.

So we bought our airline tickets
For this ancient Viscount plane
And headed out across the sea
To the land of wheat and grain.

We checked into a hostelry
And the manager turned bright red
When he realised with great surprise
There were four to every bed.

We went into the city to have a look around
But the Swedes we found
Had gone to ground
"Here we go" the only sound.

Bill had to buy a pressie
For his nagging wife Lorraine
She said if he didn't get her one
She'd be a bloody pain.

Now Gothenburg's a lovely place
A quaint old Swedish town
But one place looks like another
When the rain is pouring down.

So we headed for the stadium
The Red Army all around
And a lot were foo in the lengthy queue
As the rain came pouring down.

It wasn't long in that great red throng
When our clothes were soaking wet
But we didn't care for we were there
And there's still a few there yet!

In their famous red the Dons kicked off
The prize a magic crown
And we shouted and we bellowed
As the rain came pouring down.

In only minutes the Spaniards felt
A moment for them quite tragic
The Dons had scored and our hopes soared
A goal that was Black magic.

But our hopes were dashed as a Spaniard crashed
To the ground in the penalty box
And this Diego drew them level
As the rain ran down our socks.

But we didn't care as the Dons were there
And we knew it wouldn't be long
For Fergie and his boys in red
Were coming right on song.

And soon a dazzling dribble
From our winger Peter Weir
Had those Spaniards in a panic
And the right back feels queer.

A brilliant cross from Mark McGhee
And Real Madrid well knew it
For the ball though wet was in the net
From the head of wee John Hewitt.

And in the ground we danced around
And we banished all our fears
The Dons were going to win the cup
As we watched through joyful tears.

The ref's whistle sounded
To a roar that rent the air
And the 14,000 cheered and cried
As the rain came down their hair.

But we didn't care about the pain
Of all that soaking wind and rain
As we hugged and kissed and laughed
In a way that was quite daft.

The Dons had won the crown
In that quaint old Swedish town
They'd outplayed a famous Spanish side
That had us bursting with North East pride.

And back to bonnie Aberdeen
Our plane through the air
We sat and thought of what we'd seen
Gothenburg – WE WERE THERE.

The Dons had fire in their bellies; it was like the first leg had
damaged their reputation. The first goal arrived soon enough
for the Pittodrie faithful to sense the comeback was on – you
could feel it inside the stadium. I doubt any fan who attended

the game had any doubts the Dons would not progress to the semi-finals when Mark McGhee headed the opening goal. When he netted the second after a brilliant ball across the box from Willie Falconer in the second half I knew it would only be a matter of time before the final nail in the Ujpest coffin was hammered in.

What I didn't expect was extra time. We all knew a goal from the Hungarians meant the game was over, so the sense of trepidation was very much in evidence as the game entered the final stages. Thankfully, they never looked like scoring as the Dons controlled the game from midfield. As we entered extra time I knew another late night was in the offing. I loved the fact I would not be going to bed until well after my usual bedtime. We didn't have to wait long for Mark McGhee to score the winner. After some great build-up play between Eric Black and Gordon Strachan, the latter delivered a superb ball across the penalty area where McGhee was on hand to smash the ball home from eight yards. The roof nearly came off Pittodrie! My celebrations were wild, like many others! From that moment I knew we were through. When the full-time whistle blew, there were scenes that transported me back to the Munich game; the whole stadium was jumping. Once again the boys had conjured up something very special, to add to an ever-increasing list!

In the days preceding the semi-final draw, the talk was of a glamour tie against Manchester United or Juventus; personally I couldn't have cared less who the Dons were drawn against as I had no fear of either. Eventually, we were drawn against Portugal's Porto and I had every confidence another European final was on the cards. The first leg, away, was a close affair with the Dons defending sternly but eventually succumbing to a sucker punch when a cleverly worked corner kick caught the Dons defence napping. It ended 1–0 and I clearly recall saying to Dad while reading the report over breakfast the next morning that we had come from behind before, surely we could do it again. Dad said we should go to the second leg at Pittodrie as it had the makings of another memorable night. He was quite right, but for all the wrong reasons.

The 25th April 1984 was a damp, cold day – school went by in a flash! I was unable to concentrate, much to the annoyance of my teachers. At break time Ewan and I talked about the game and plotted Aberdeen's victory. The final was set for Basel in Switzerland and we both prematurely looked forward to another European adventure, hopefully with a luxury bus in tow! As was the norm in those days I would get home from school, crack on with my meaningless homework, have dinner, jump in the bath and get ready for the game. Dad would arrive home from work early, grab a bite to eat and gather us all into the car making sure Ewan and I were adequately wrapped up to protect us from the strong wind blowing over from the North Sea. As we made our way into Pittodrie Dad sat us closer to the pitch, an unusual step. Dad's persona that night was different; I sensed nervousness from him. It made me uncomfortable. Did he know something that I didn't?

Pittodrie was covered in a blanket of fog; I struggled to see the far side goal by the Merkland Stand and complained to Dad who continued to sit quietly as the game edged back and forth. Aberdeen faced a well-organised Porto side and despite dominating possession, the Dons could not find a way through. The first half passed without incident and Pittodrie was quiet. The second half began very much like the first had ended with Porto defending deep and the Dons struggling to create any chances of note. Then the inconceivable happened, I remember Porto's Silva picking the ball up just inside the Dons half and making a beeline towards goal. He managed to evade a couple of challenges; someone from behind me yelled, "Take him down." Out the corner of my eye I noticed Jim Leighton had left his line but I couldn't see properly, with the fog thick in front of my eyes and people in front of us standing for a better look.

As Silva edged closer, we were all trying to see the action. I thought I saw the ball go over the head of Jim Leighton: I held my breath, then silence! A gasp fell over Pittodrie and a muffled cheer rose up from the far side of the Main Stand; I could see Silva running towards them, arms aloft. "Oh my God, they've scored!" It took a few seconds for my brain to compute what this meant; I looked at Dad who by this point was slumped in his seat with his head in his hands. 2–0 down with an away goal, the Dons needed to score three in the last 15 minutes.

Ewan and I sat down and looked at each other blankly; we knew there and then the Dons were going out! It was a horrible feeling; I was numb. The closing stages of the game went by slowly as the disappointment sank deeper. We went home in complete silence. Once home Mum met us at the door and immediately grabbed Dad and starting sobbing. I looked on slightly perplexed, I knew we had lost but did it justify Mum crying? They held each other for what seemed like an age. The next morning we sat quietly reading the papers and discussing the game. I could still sense the huge disappointment with both Mum and Dad as they chatted about the night before. I soon forgot about it, as I knew the Dons were only a handful of games away from winning the league.

I would subsequently learn many years later while on a trip with Dad into the Highlands of Scotland that ahead of the second leg he had arranged a train to take the Aberdeen fans to Basel for the final. He told me this was done in haste after the first leg as he had every confidence the Dons could turn the tie on its head. I listened on, gobsmacked. It turned out a train would take the fans from Aberdeen direct to Felixstowe, on to France to be met by another train, a quick transfer and another train all the way to Basel in Switzerland. Dad told me he sold the train out, took hundreds of pounds worth of deposits and would have made an astonishing £60,000 profit!

For a few moments I was speechless. I asked Dad why it had taken him many years to tell me the story and he explained, as a ten-year-old, I was in no position to understand the huge impact financially that sort of money would have had on our lives but as an adult I was in a position to fully appreciate exactly what it meant! I truly was astonished and picked his brains for the rest of the trip. £60,000 was a life-changing sum back in 1984, no doubt it would have offered the chance to make us more financially stable as a family (not that we ever struggled to be fair), pay off the mortgage and keep me in the finest pair of football boots money could buy!

Which brings me nicely to a topic which I think needs to be addressed and quickly for the sake of our beloved game going forward – money! To be clear from the off, I bear no grudges whatsoever to the money top players earn today. I say good luck to them but I do believe some common sense has to be adhered to sooner rather than later, and wage caps need to be introduced, otherwise we are in serious danger of this spiralling out of control. Just look at the debts some clubs have incurred over the years. In fact, look no further than the Scottish Premier League and the problems to befall Rangers and Hearts! Yes, many of their problems are self-inflicted and poorly managed, so let's not make this a trend.

Once upon a time, footballers would travel to a match on the same bus as the fans. Today, they're more likely to own the bus company. When a player can earn more in a month than many fans will earn in their entire working life, you have to start wondering how fans can possibly engage with them on any level. I understand the marketing pull of a host of players, Beckham, Ronaldo, Messi and so on, and the revenue they generate for their individual clubs but come on, £300,000 a week for Wayne Rooney! Really??

Should it matter what these guys are paid? It's worth pausing to relate it to everyday life. The average person's salary in England is £25,000 a year. In Spain, its £19,000 a year – but unemployment there is 24.6% and, crucially for football fans, it's more than twice that for the under 25s – 53%. So, it's not just a question of why they're still watching these millionaires kick a ball about but how on earth are they affording it?? I honestly don't know how the average fan affords to go to games in the modern era. A good day out at a top English club will cost you going on £150, if not more, by the time the tickets have been purchased, a matchday programme has been read, a bite to eat and a drink, and that's before the petrol has been put in the car or the bus/train fare has been paid for. Sometimes I wonder if professional footballers should think more on this when pulling on his shirt.

During my time with Celtic TV I enjoyed the company of many a Lisbon Lion (Celtic's 1967 European Cup-winning side) and often wondered why they don't profit from the name "Lisbon Lions": they changed the face of Scottish and British football by becoming the first team from the British Isles to win the European Cup. They are an important part of our game and its coveted history and should be honoured in the right manner. Yes, they have a stand named after them at Celtic Park but that's not enough in my opinion, they should all profit from any merchandise sold off the back of the name; they should all own it and have the profits shared equally amongst themselves and their immediate families – is this too much to ask?

Ask any players from that era, or the 1970s and 1980s, all they wanted professionally was to win! Winning WAS the attitude back then, they wanted to win, they wanted the bragging rights over their peers, they wanted to showcase what they had won, and rightly so. Don't show me how many mock Tudor mansions you own. How many Range Rovers you drive, or yachts you holiday on. I don't care how many celebrity girlfriends fall off your arm; I will judge you by your medals and honours. Willie Miller recently told me when he played all he wanted to do was win. He never cared for the celebrity side of the business. He told me from the moment Sir Alex Ferguson arrived at the club he instilled a winning mentality. Sir Alex demanded success, and with that would come fame and adulation. All the players in Fergie's era wanted nothing more than to collect trophies and medals; it is how these players were ultimately judged.

How many players can we say that of now? Not many in my book; look at Chris Maguire, Fraser Fyvie and more recently Ryan Fraser. In my opinion all these boys left the club prematurely. Money, bad agents and possibly a touch of arrogance clouded their judgement. Stay and win and finish your education first, then think about the financial implications as you mature. That would be my advice! Too many young players these days judge their levels of success on how many friends they have on Facebook, and how many people follow them on Twitter.

If I could offer one more snippet of advice to all the top players in England I would suggest an internet search of two chaps by the names Sam Chisholm and David Hill who, between them, negotiated the first-ever Premiership television deal, which ultimately flooded the English game with millions of pounds. This is merely a wee thought on my behalf! Looking back on it now I fully understand why Dad was so nervous ahead of the Porto game, his quiet demeanour during the game and the reaction from Mum afterwards! What a story, and what a shame! That game against Porto holds differing emotions for obvious reasons but I will also never forget it for another reason. It was the only game I ever caught the ball during a match!

Over the years the Dons have offered me a variety of emotions, which only come from being a football fan. I, of course, have had my fair share of the very best moments since 1981 but never did I expect to have the most terrifying experience of my life just a few yards away from the stadium. It was January 3rd 1984. We had just enjoyed a wonderful family Christmas and New Year and I was very much looking forward to the Dons taking on St Johnstone.

I recall travelling from Newburgh to Aberdeen along the A94, which in those days was a single-track road all the way into town. The snow had started to fall gently in the morning and I couldn't help but think how much I wanted more so I could go sledging after the game. As we always did back in the early 1980s, we parked the car along the beach front, directly opposite the Kings Links Golf Course. Mum made sure I was adequately wrapped up and gave Angus strict instructions to keep my scarf tight and my gloves firmly mummified over my hands. Dad, Mum and Peter made their way round to the

South Stand as Angus and I trotted along Pittodrie Street, past the Main Stand and into Merkland Road to take our seats in the Paddock.

Going into this game, the Dons were Kings of Europe having just added the Super Cup to the already polished Cup Winners' Cup and were unbeaten in the league in eleven. The opening 45 minutes against St Johnstone will go down – in my opinion – as the finest display from any Aberdeen team I have watched over the years. They were simply outstanding. 3–0 up at the break thanks to goals from Gordon Strachan, an Eric Black volley, and a particular peach from Dougie Bell, I sat on in awe watching this superlative display of how football should be played. The Saints players must have been delighted when half-time eventually arrived, if anything to give them some sort of respite from the ongoing slaughter.

During the break Angus and I queued for warm Bovril and a pie, which on a bitterly cold afternoon like this was like feasting on the finest banquet. The snow continued to fall lightly but in no way, shape, or form did I anticipate what was about to unfold. All of a sudden the power went out and Pittodrie was engulfed in darkness. An awkward cheer echoed around the now still stadium. As quickly as they went out the lights returned and blinded Pittodrie for a moment.

At this point it started to get interesting. For those of you who attended the game you will appreciate exactly the story I am telling, for those of you who weren't there please allow your imagination to run riot. This is Aberdeen meeting Hollywood blockbuster *The Day After Tomorrow*. From almost out of nothing a blizzard hit Pittodrie and the surrounding areas. Within a matter of minutes the pitch was covered in a thick layer of snow. I watched on not quite believing my eyes as the fall became heavier and heavier. It wasn't long before I couldn't see the Beach End. Angus and I sat in silence but some gave up the ghost and decided to head home. After a quick inspection by the referee the announcement was made that the game would be abandoned, much to the annoyance of the many disgruntled fans. We now had no choice but to make our way back to the car. As we came out the Paddock I held on tightly to Angus's jacket. I could feel the wind battering me from all angles and the cold air pinching my face, but I had no fear as the stadium served as our protector.

Once out in the open I was shocked at the force of the driving wind and aggressive blizzard, which almost felt biblical. I grabbed Angus by the arm hoping he would lead me across the links. We trudged our way through the snow towards the prom, the wind whipping my face. I was now in pain and tried to move my scarf up round my face but this proved laborious and I gave up. As we edged closer to the embankment I had lost all sense of direction, I lifted my head to see where we were but was met by a swarm of pain as the snow punched me over and over again. Angus did his best to reassure me that all would be OK, and not to worry, but I was starting to feel a little frightened. He looked around but saw nothing except a few struggling souls on their own expedition. Angus led me to some whin bushes where, much to my relief, we managed to shelter for a short while. I was now worried about Mum, Dad and Peter and hoped they were all fine, especially Peter.

After resting for a few moments Angus said, "Come on, let's get to the top." We literally climbed up the embankment on our hands and knees. My jeans at this point were soaking from the driving snow, my hands almost frozen, fingers hurting, and bones aching. Just a little bit further and surely the car would be in sight. Now I truly was frightened, once at the top the force of the wind caught me unprepared and pinned me against a car. I screamed to Angus, as by now I was genuinely petrified. I looked along the road but saw nothing then out of the chaos a guiding hand, a strong hand, a hand I recognised. It was Dad! I caught his eye. Dad must have sensed my fear as he took a firm hold of me, held me tight to his body and guided us all to the car.

Once at the car we all fell in, one after the other. I clearly recall Peter, Angus, his Mum Betty and I cowering in the back as I pleaded with Dad to get the heater on. I was so cold and so scared I could not stop shaking, Betty put her arm round me and I relaxed as the heat started to flow through my body, "please get me home Dad" I said as he looked through his mirror at me and gave me that reassuring smile of his. Thankfully, it didn't take long for us to negotiate our way home but like many villages in the area we were starved of power for a number of days, which at the time was quite novel, but a nightmare for my poor parents.

Gordon Strachan told me during one of our many chats that he was without hot water for two weeks and poor Billy Stark, who was suffering from a hip injury that fateful day, attempted to drive down south to see a specialist but was stranded in a gridlock for many hours near Perth as the snow battered the country from top to bottom. Recently, I took in a game on a trip back to Salzburg to visit Miriam's parents; Red Bull v Lech Poznan in the Europa League. That night Miriam's brother, Michael, and I sat in −14°C watching utter shite and I could not help but cast my mind back to the St Johnstone game and allow myself the odd smile here and there as I remembered the experience. Typically, I missed the only goal of the game inside the Red Bull Arena as I was away spending a penny, which I had to snap off, it was that frigging cold!

When the 1983/84 Scottish Cup campaign began, I started to take success for granted. As an 11-year-old I had rarely experienced defeat and expected the side to continue where they had left off the previous season. We attended the Kilmarnock and Dundee United games at Pittodrie, both matches going to a replay before the Dons progressed to the semi-finals. For the first time I had to be content with a semi away from Hampden, this time a round trip to the capital. I had never been to Tynecastle before so I was particularly looking forward to this one. I had no doubt the Dons would beat Dundee as, on paper, the side were miles ahead in terms of experience, skill and success. When we arrived at the home of Hearts I was dismayed to discover so many fans surrounded us that I couldn't see. Fortunately, a couple of lads kindly gave up their spot by the barrier so I perched myself on top, leaning against Dad for safety. Ian Porteous and Gordon Strachan scored the goals in a scrappy 2–0 win and we went home happy in the knowledge that another trip to Hampden was in the offing.

For the final itself, Dad took the unusual step of taking us down to Glasgow on the train. We left Aberdeen station early Friday afternoon, lost in the thousands with the same idea. I actually enjoyed the train as we could relax and Peter and I could enjoy our favourite pastime, spotting as many football stadiums as possible en route. The banter and the beer were in full flow on the train and I think a few lads were slightly worse for wear by the time we reached Queen Street. The following morning was a fairly manic affair, as we had to catch a lift with Bobby Maitland, a colleague of my grandpa's. Bobby was reporting on the game and very kindly organised our tickets. As was the norm by now, we arrived at Hampden in plenty of time.

May 9th 1984 was the date for the 99th Scottish Cup Final and fittingly it was Scotland's form sides contesting the country's premier cup competition. Celtic, who had won the trophy on 26 previous occasions, faced the Dons, who were only appearing in their 11th final. For the first time, I felt apprehensive ahead of such an occasion; Celtic were an excellent side with many formidable players. The first thing that struck me when we were hanging about outside Hampden was the colour; everywhere we looked it was a sea of green and white. Thousands of Celtic fans were making their way to their respective turnstiles, tricolours flying high, waving back and forth in the wind. It was an awe-inspiring scene but it did nothing for my nerves.

As we took our seats in the Main Stand, you won't be surprised to learn we were seated among the Celtic fans! This part of cup final day was beginning to do my head in! By then, I really wanted to be among the Red Army, shout and scream, sing the club songs and enjoy the company of fellow Dandies. Aberdeen started the game fairly well and it was no surprise when they took the lead thanks to a spectacular scissor kick from Eric Black. I was out my seat like a shot as were the Celtic fans that complained Eric was in an offside position. I quickly re-took mine and smiled at Dad, who winked back. The defining moment that some argued changed the pattern of the game arrived not long before half-time when Roy Aitken was sent off for a cynical foul on Mark McGhee. The Bear was my least favourite of all the Celtic players and I was delighted he would take no further part in the game.

How ironic that, years later, I would get to know Roy as an adult and discover what a true gentleman he is, not at all like the preconceived views I had of him as a youngster. During the second half the lads appeared to take their foot off the pedal, which offered Celtic a way back into the game. As the full-time whistle edged ever closer, a few sorry souls were making their way to the exits thinking their beloved Hoops had blown it. Out of nothing Paul McStay smashed an equaliser past Jim Leighton and the very same sorry souls re-appeared feeling much happier. To be honest, I wasn't overly concerned when the game went to extra time as I had yet to see the side lose in the ensuing 30 minutes. Fergie made a couple of changes for the extra period, introducing Billy Stark and Dougie Bell to the action. The change had the desired effect when after Dougie's 25-yard shot smashed off the woodwork; Gordon Strachan picked up the loose ball and crossed to an unmarked Mark McGhee at the back post. Mark's volley was perfection personified and the lads were back in the lead. It was a great moment, the few Dons fans around us jumping up and down with glee, the Red Army away to our left in raptures.

The Dons held on and clinched their third successive Scottish Cup, the first team to do so since Rangers in the 1930s, and again in the 1960s. It was another wonderful achievement. The trip was made all the better by the fact that on our way home on the train the next day, Mark McGhee was sitting a couple of rows down from us. Naturally, I asked him to sign my matchday programme. It was McGhee's last game for the club and he was off to SV Hamburg in the Bundesliga. I told him I didn't want him to leave but he said it was time to go and not to worry, as more great players would join the club soon. He was extremely charming and had no problems chatting to a wee kid pestering him for an autograph, another nice memento from a memorable trip.

Always a first time ...

The League Cup, up until 1985, offered me little in terms of success. As most people know, Alex Ferguson cursed the trophy with his own utterance saying; "It wasn't as important as others." For a few years these words would come back to haunt him. When the Dons lost to Airdrie the day after my 12th birthday I started to wonder if I would ever see the Dons win this competition. Little did I know when Aberdeen faced Ayr United in the second round, ten years later the League Cup would have a profound effect on my life.

Having disposed of St Johnstone and Hearts without too much bother, the Dons faced Dundee United in the semis. The New Firm was by now very much established in Scottish football and giving the Old Firm a run for their money. I feared Jim McLean's Dundee United, always had done from an early age. United appeared to be a bogey team for the Dons in the competition – to me at least – and on more than one occasion since I started supporting the Reds, knocked Aberdeen out. Now that I was in secondary school Mum and Dad had no problems with me attending midweek games. Angus drove us into town in his clapped-out luminous green Vauxhall Astra Mark One.

I was feeling nervous about the game, even though Eric Black had given the Dons a slender one-goal lead from the first game at Tannadice. Like most New Firm games in the mid 1980s, apart from the odd one or two they were mostly tight affairs and the second game at Pittodrie was no different. In front of a near-capacity crowd, the Dons progressed to the final thanks to a solitary Frank McDougall goal.

On the way home I asked Angus if he could arrange with Dad to get tickets for the final and see if we could all make the trip, an idea which I believe he quite fancied. Upon arriving home Dad was ready for me, and my barrage of questions. As per usual, he answered them all the same, "we'll see". I went to my bed a happy camper. Thankfully, I only had to wait a few days for the good news with Dad securing four tickets for the final, courtesy of my uncle Bill.

Awaiting Aberdeen in the final at Hampden on October 27th was Hibs. I was feeling so confident about this game that probably for the first time I didn't feel any apprehension or nerves ahead of the match. With all due respect to Hibs, who had performed a minor miracle to get to the final, I saw them as nothing but a pushover! As was the Begg way, we made our way to Glasgow the day before the game by car and stayed with gran and grandpa in Bishopbriggs. With my understanding of the game developing and knack for picking up on things as I matured improving, listening to grandpa on the phone as he set to work his small team of reporters ahead of the game became more and more interesting. I would sit outside his office eavesdropping on his conversations with fellow journalists hoping to hear a snippet of team news or anything related to the Dons.

He knew I was outside listening in and at times would pop his head round the corner, meet my eye, and offer me his lovely smile. A smile which I miss every day! With his vast knowledge of the game I always asked him for a prediction but he would never offer one. What he would do is wink at me and say; "Anything can happen on the day son." Even though my darling grandpa has been dead going on 25 years, I can still vividly see him in my mind leaving the house. He always gave my gran a small peck on the cheek before getting into his old blue Nissan Talbot. He always dressed the same. The very smartest of suits money can buy; polished shoes, leather suitcase, raincoat and an old-fashioned gentleman's hat! He was one of a kind and I doubt the world of football journalism in Scotland has been the same since he died. In the early days he always led the way so on a dreary day we made our way to Hampden. I was so looking forward to the match. I couldn't wait to sample the atmosphere. Once inside the stadium we took our seats in the Main Stand on the far left. Away to my left the Red Army packed the terraces. As the teams warmed up Peter and I tucked into a newly purchased meat pie, a small treat only reserved for special occasions.

When the game started I knew from the off we had too much for Hibs. It wasn't long before we were all celebrating. From a brilliant counter-attack involving Frank McDougall and a mazy run from John Hewitt, Eric Black headed the Dons into the lead. Peter and I were off our seats before the ball hit the back of the net. Peter by now was starting to understand football and he was jumping up and down like the rest of us.

When the second went in almost directly in line with where we were sitting it was time to sit back and watch the Dons at their best. John Hewitt floated in an inviting cross, this time with his right foot and Billy Stark, who was by now cementing his place in the Dons' midfield, glanced a superb header home. I think Dad in particular enjoyed well-worked goals and he was up applauding another fine effort, 2–0, game over, before 15 minutes were on the clock.

For the rest of the game the Dons controlled the midfield with Willie Miller and Alex McLeish bossing from the back. Having not conceded throughout the tournament I had no fears that the Dons would keep a clean sheet. When Eric

Black scored the third and decisive goal it was time to relax and enjoy the atmosphere. It was rare to enjoy the closing stages of a cup final as over the years all my experiences had been tense affairs, not this time though as we sat and chatted, laughed and offered the odd song here and there.

When the full-time whistle blew we all stood and applauded. Peter and I stood on our seats to get a better view and when Willie turned our way to lift the Skol/League Cup high into the Hampden sky we all cheered and sang along with the remaining Dons fans. We drove home with our scarves flying out the back of the car, happy in the knowledge we had seen another final as a family, and yet to taste defeat. I started to believe the Begg family was the Dons' lucky charm and we would continue to support the lads from the terraces, come hell or high water.

The end of an era

When the 1986 Scottish Cup campaign began, I was desperate for the Dons to do well. The previous season, I had tasted defeat in the competition for the first time when Aberdeen lost 2–1 to Dundee United at Tynecastle in the semi-final. The feeling was horrible; I went to bed after the game and cried! In the early rounds, there had been evidence that this might not be the Dons' year; performance levels were well below par. Although Montrose were dealt with fairly comfortably at Pittodrie, Arbroath at Gayfield offered a slightly stiffer test with Joe Miller putting us through by a solitary goal.

In the quarters, the Dons needed a replay at Pittodrie to overcome a very stubborn Dundee side. Thank goodness Peter Weir was on hand to send the Dons through to yet another semi-final where we would face Hibs at Dens Park. We drove down to Dundee on the day of the game. Like many other fans we arrived in plenty of time, found a good spot in the ground and relished the pre-game atmosphere. The lads were on fire that day and easily brushed aside the Edinburgh club in an impressive 3–0 win. The journey home was great fun too as we passed many Dons fans on the A96, beeping horns and waving at everyone.

In the weeks leading up to the final I asked Dad to arrange the tickets for the Aberdeen end, as I was desperate to be amongst our own and feel at ease while watching the game. He told me not to worry; "famous last words", I quietly thought to myself.

May 10th 1986 was a truly beautiful day but I recall feeling very apprehensive. We travelled to Hampden with my grandpa and chilled out before making our way into the stadium. I was looking forward to being seated with the Red Army but when we got to our seats, it wasn't a red and white scene that greeted us but a maroon-and-white one. Once again we were sat with the opposing fans! I was really upset and wondered if we were ever destined to sit in the Aberdeen end.

The Hearts fans were hurting after a dramatic last-day collapse at the hands of Dundee, which handed Celtic the league title after the Hoops had hammered St Mirren 5–0 at Love Street! I was certainly expecting some form of backlash from the Jam Tarts but once the game got underway my nerves settled down and I started to relax. The Dons had the better of the opening stages. We didn't have to wait too long for the opening goal. John Hewitt collected a superb through ball from Willie Miller and he smashed a drive past the diving Henry Smith from 20 yards; 1–0 to the Dons. As I celebrated, Mum pulled me back down to my seat in a swift move which caught me by surprise. She was obviously conscious of the company we were keeping. I wasn't particularly fussed. What did the Hearts fans expect? That I should just sit back and applaud politely? Come on!

It was soon obvious to me, after a very long season, Hearts had nothing left in their tank. The league campaign had taken the wind out of their sails and they rarely troubled the Aberdeen defence. The second half could not have started better for Alex Ferguson's men as a wonderful cross from Peter Weir was superbly dummied by Frank McDougall and John Hewitt made no mistake from a couple of yards. Superb move, wonderful goal! I remained seated but hugged both Mum and Dad as we celebrated quietly. If we managed to contain our emotions for the second goal, the third and decisive strike was celebrated in the correct and proper manner. Peter Weir's free kick found the head of Billy Stark who dived full-length to guide a superb header into the back of the net, a truly glorious goal. 3–0, game over.

That goal by Billy was my Dad's favourite Aberdeen goal of all time. I asked Billy to contribute to this book by telling me about that moment. This is what he had to say:

"The goal in 1986 is still pretty vivid (as is the one which was scandalously chalked off!). It was provided by my old mate Peter Weir from a free kick in the out-side-left position. It was an out-swinger and a couple of players challenged for it just in front of me. It evaded them and I dived full length to connect and put it back into the far corner of the net. A couple of early lessons contributed to the goal and they stood me in good stead throughout my career.

"My father always told me when I was in the penalty box to anticipate defenders missing the ball and be ready to capitalise. And a manager by the name of Ferguson told me when the ball came across goal, to head it back where it came from – see, easy! It was, as you can imagine, a fantastic feeling to score in a Scottish Cup Final and, of course, when I look back now, it completed the 'double', having scored in the Skol Cup Final earlier in the season, something no Aberdeen player had done. I still have the jersey in my loft – we didn't swap in those days! The medal is in a case alongside the others, also tucked away in the loft!"

By the time the full-time whistle sounded, most of the Hearts fans had already left. I actually felt really sorry for them as their side had promised so much but delivered very little. As Willie Miller climbed the steps to receive the trophy Dad allowed me to stand on the seat so I could have a good view of the team holding the cup aloft. It was a pretty cool moment as the team was only a few yards away from us. After all the usual post-match celebrations died down and all the fans had exited the stadium, we made our way down to the main entrance to greet my grandpa. To my delight, the team was making its way on to the bus so I ran around the side and managed to pester Jim Leighton, Billy Stark and John Hewitt for their autographs. How was I to know at that time I would have to wait four years for my next Scottish Cup Final?

That same year Sir Alex Ferguson began a journey, which ultimately changed the face of English football as we know it. In November 1986, Sir Alex took up the reins at Manchester United after the sacking of Ron Atkinson. When the news officially reached the local media it dominated the column inches, radio and TV stations for weeks. Aberdeen had lost their greatest-ever manager to one of the biggest clubs in the world, a sleeping giant!

I could not quite believe what I was reading, hearing and watching when faced with the devastating news. As a maturing 14-year-old I had a fair understanding of the game, and the trappings it offered, but I was not expecting Sir Alex to leave. It came as a terrible shock. I wondered where the Dons would go from here, who would be the new manager, would the players follow suit? When he left, it felt like the club, in fact the city, was in mourning. The next game at Pittodrie had a subdued feel to it; the place was quiet, almost eerie. Collectively, as fans, we were all lost in our own thoughts. You don't need me to tell you Aberdeen FC has not been the same since Fergie left all those years ago.

I didn't really know what to expect after he left to be honest. I think in my youthful innocence I expected things to carry on as normal. Alex McLeish said that some players were delighted when he left but went on to miss him soon afterwards. His presence, his desire, his drive, his passion, his anger – his everything – had gone and I believe it has never been replaced despite the greatest efforts from all those who proceeded him. Ian Porterfield did his best but had a near impossible job. Should the board have appointed a bigger name? Should they have appointed a Scotsman at the time? I believe they should have. Alex Smith and Jocky Scott did a fantastic job but failed when it mattered the most. Willie Miller should have been given more time. Big Roy Aitken did not have enough experience as a manager. Alex Miller, Paul Hegarty and Ebbe Skovdahl had disastrous spells in charge. Steve Paterson should never have been appointed in my opinion. Jimmy Calderwood worked wonders. Mark McGhee, as much as it pains me to say, almost brought us to our knees. Craig Brown restored parity. I think no matter who sits behind the manager's desk at Pittodrie they have to fully acknowledge, whether they like it or not, fans of our club especially, of my age and generation, still believe deep down that maybe one day the glory days will greet us again. This is what faces them every day when they walk through the corridors of Pittodrie – I wonder who is up for the challenge?!

Champions

Of all the chapters and stories I have written in this book, defining winning the league championship was the most difficult of all. To be honest I don't have much to say. I've been to hundreds of games around Scotland following the Dons hoping that one day a title would be delivered, our first since 1985. Alas, we've never really come close since season 1990/91. I don't want to particularly bore you with tales of what games I went to and what happened, I'll leave that for the historians. All that's left to write about is my own experiences when the Dons actually won the league, which is only twice – believe it or not!

Since 1981, when I first started supporting the Dons, I was still getting to grips with the game and how it worked. Early on I had no conception of what a league championship was and, more importantly, what it meant. Having watched videos of Alex Ferguson comically run across the Easter Road pitch to congratulate his band of men a few years previously, I had an inkling his actions meant something, but to what degree I was relatively unsure. Dad had done his very best to explain to me on numerous occasions how the game worked and what the Scottish Premier League stood for. But, as the Dons had only won in nearly all the cup competitions they had entered since I started following the side, I understood this to be more important. However, that mindset would soon change over the coming years.

Coming into season 1983/84 I was a regular at Pittodrie, and had been for the past two seasons. Mum and Dad allowed me the grace of attending most games with Angus in the Merkland Stand, while they took their seats in the South Stand. I loved being in the Paddock. I was in the heart of the stadium as far as I was concerned. I learned all the songs from the pocket of fans who always sat in the same area, even those with the odd naughty word or two! Those songs were only ever reserved for days out at Pittodrie, or the occasional away trip. I knew all the words to every song; "The Northern Lights of old Aberdeen", "a European Song" (Aberdeen's Cup Winner's Cup Final song) which had been purchased and played on loop on my old record player over and over and over again. Much to the annoyance of Mum, Dad and Peter may I add. "One Willie Miller, there's only one Wille Miller" reverberated throughout the Begg household for years. I always enjoyed the odd rendition of "you're shit and you know you are, you're shit and you know you are". It was so naughty. But yet a little fun. I daren't ever sing it in front of Mum and Dad and Angus's mum Betty. I refrained from singing songs which included the word f**k, or words to that effect, as I knew this was stepping too close to the mark. I thank the lord my Mum is relatively out of harm's way when the Dons lose in this day and age. The same can't be said of my poor work colleagues, though, who have to endure many an expletive on a Saturday afternoon!

Having won the Super Cup at the tail-end of 1983 I couldn't wait for the New Year and all the excitement it would bring. I desperately wanted the Dons to win the league; I was yet to taste success as Scottish champions and wanted to know how it felt. Would I feel as exhilarated as May 11th, would I have that sense of utter joy as I did when watching Dad celebrate Mark McGhee's winner against Hamburg only a few months before? All the answers to my questions would be delivered on May 2nd 1984 when the Dons faced Hearts at Tynecastle knowing a win would secure the league title.

In the weeks leading up to the game the Dons were in magnificent form, losing only once in the league all year. We watched the side demolish New Firm rivals Dundee United 5-1 at Pittodrie in the middle of March, enjoying two rare goals for big Doug Rougvie. Dad had helped me work out if the Dons continued their winning run the title could potentially be wrapped up against Hearts. As much as this excited me I was slightly disappointed, I wanted to physically be there to watch the Dons win it. If maximum points were secured from here on in I would miss out! I actually hoped for maybe a draw in the next couple of games, which would mean the Dons facing Hibs at Pittodrie knowing victory would mean the glory of being crowned Scottish champions once again! Typically, the Dons were unstoppable and beat St Johnstone twice, and Dundee, en route. My date with destiny meant a night sitting at home listening to the bleeding radio!

As per usual I couldn't concentrate at school, I wanted to get home, finish my homework and prepare for an exciting night ahead. Listening to a game on the radio, at times, gives you a false sense of perspective. I always struggled to get a real feel for the game and how the Dons were playing. Dad was listening while pottering about the house. I kept asking him how the game was going and he told me to relax, "They're doing just fine," he said. When the half-time whistle blew I was fairly upbeat. The Dons started the second half brightly but Hearts continued to be the better side, creating the odd chance here and there with the BBC commentator describing Jim Leighton as the Dons man of the match so far. With half an hour left to play the Begg household exploded into life! From a long throw the ball fell kindly to the feet of Stuart

McKimmie. The commentator described how he made room for himself and with a left-foot drive the ball hit the back of the net! "YEEESSSS" I screamed at the top of my voice, I could hear the Dons fans in the background roaring with delight. I ran downstairs and hugged Dad, "we're going to win now aren't we" I said. Dad just smiled, Mum patted my head. I skipped back up to my room to listen to the rest of the game. Thankfully, the Dons controlled the game with Jim Leighton making one or two more important saves along the way.

The full-time whistle blew and Aberdeen were champions! I was so happy but at the same time a tad down as I missed out. Not to worry as the following season all worked out just fine!

"You're extremely calm, usually you're a nervous wreck, what's wrong with you?" Angus was right, I wasn't nervous at all as we made our way across the golf links to Pittodrie. "I'm not worried – today, we'll win the league again." Angus smiled at my youthful prediction as we carried on walking round to the Merkland Stand full of the joys of life, as if something very special was about to bestow our afternoon. The strange thing was, today of all days, I wasn't concerned at all. Even though the Dons were facing their nearest challengers Celtic, I had every confidence the point would be secured to retain the league title. In fact, I fully expected the Dons to soundly beat Celtic. Having supported Aberdeen the past few years, I expected nothing less, why should I? I had seen Alex Ferguson's side lift the Scottish Cup twice, the Cup Winners' Cup, the Super Cup, and win the league the previous year. Come 4.45pm on Saturday 27th April 1985, I would be celebrating again.

A few weeks prior to the Celtic game, as we sat in the Paddock watching another masterful performance from the

Dons as they beat Dundee United 4–2 with two cracking goals from John Hewitt, Angus turned to me and said "if we win today and the next couple of games, and Celtic continue to win their games, we can win the league against them in three weeks". This excited me. I so desperately wanted to watch the Dons win the title. Angus showed me the league table in the programme and explained what needed to be done. I listened on intently as the pieces of the puzzle came together. Unlike last season I sensed this was destiny and all would work out just fine, the script was written.

Making our way into the stadium on that glorious afternoon I could hear the Celtic fans in the Beach End singing away. I was always captivated by the colour and mass of Hoops fans that made their way up the road from Glasgow. The sight of green and white always impressed me; to be honest, it still does today. We took our place on the old wooden benches, halfway down the Paddock, just to the right of the goal. We had the perfect view. I could sense a little nervousness from the Dons fans but as the teams warmed up ahead of the game the atmosphere turned to one of excitement. Pittodrie was packed, all around us folk were chit-chattering away, talking about the game, the team Fergie was going to pick, the Celtic side. There was a loud hum with kick-off just a few minutes away.

A favourite pre-match ritual was the announcement of the teams by the Pittodrie PA. As he read out player by player each was greeted with a large cheer. I always reserved my biggest and loudest for Willie Miller, Peter Weir and my new-found hero Frank McDougall. Frank had been added to the squad the previous summer and was an instant hit with the Dons fans. His hat-trick against Rangers on a cold miserable January day offered the former St Mirren man cult status

among the Dons faithful. His predatory instincts inside the
six-yard box made him almost unstoppable. His contribution
that season should not be underestimated. As the Celtic team
was being read out a very loud chorus of boos greeted each
one. As the PA did his best to read out the Celtic side over the
raucous home crowd a spine-tingling rendition of "here we go"
reverberated around Pittodrie, it seemed the whole stadium bar
the Beach End joined in. The noise level reached a new time high
for me as the teams ran out onto the pitch.

Immediately, I was up on my feet, waving my scarf high
above my head as all around clapped and cheered the Dons
onto the park. Jim Leighton, as he always did, ran towards
us clapping both hands above his head. He placed his spare
gloves deep inside the goal, looked towards the Paddock one
last time, and pumped his fists. This was just the tonic the
Aberdeen fans needed as all around us shouts of "come on"
and "get intae them" shook the foundations of the Paddock.
I was loving it. Pittodrie was bouncing! The Dons started
the game brightly, keeping control of the ball in midfield and
holding Celtic at bay. The Dons created good chances with
Stuart McKimmie, Billy Stark and big Frank all coming close.
I suspected half-time to come with the teams locked at 0–0.
My suspicion floundered when out of almost nothing Celtic
took the lead.

After some brilliant trickery by striker Frank McGarvey he
delivered a cross to the back stick. I watched Mo Johnston and
Billy Stark go up to challenge for the ball. Much to my relief it
fell to safety but out the corner of my eye I noticed Mo Johnston
with his hand in the air. What was he doing? I looked at Angus,
who had his eye on the ref. I was a little confused, and then
unbelievably he pointed to the spot!! I couldn't believe it, I had
to stand on the bench just to see what was going on. I grabbed

Developing my skills from an early age, Glasgow 1973

Peter and I getting ready for a
Scotland v England game,
Gunton Hall 1980

Christmas 1982

Top: Enjoying Christmas with Mum's side of the family, Dorchester 1984

Above left: Ready in plenty of time for the 1983 Scottish Cup Final, feeling very confident another trophy will be delivered

Above right: Awaiting the Scottish Cup Final 1984

Left: Carefully preparing another team poster for my bedroom wall – must not de-face Willie Miller when removing the staple! Newburgh 1987

Dad and me playing football

Grandpa outside the old Scottish Football Association offices,
Park Circus, Glasgow 1980

Enjoying a family holiday in Tenerife 1988, upon returning home
I was dealt the biggest blow of them all

Team photograph with the Arsenal Ex-Professional and Celebrity XI
before a charity match at Highbury – June 1997

Two previously unseen
Bad Boys Inc photos

From my days at Models 1

Meeting Sir Alex Ferguson two days after joining Manchester United TV, co-presenter Jeannie B delivering some glamour to the proceedings, July 1999

Here I am with the Manchester United trophies following the Treble after embarking on my sports broadcasting career in 1999

One of my fondest memories during my time with MUTV spending a day at Aberdeen FC filming for a one-off documentary with first team coach Tommy Moller Nielsen, May 2000

Aberdeen legend Teddy Scott and I putting the world to rights in his Aladdin's cave of football memorabilia at Pittodrie, March 2000

Angus, leant on his shoulder, and he looked at me and said "they've got a penalty". I slumped back down. As quickly as I was down I had to stand back up as all around strained for sight of the looming penalty kick. I tried to get some leverage by again leaning on Angus's shoulder. Now I could see. Jim Leighton, by now, was bent over, smacking his hands. My eyes darted from him to Roy Aitken and back again. Jim, now bouncing gently on the balls of his feet, arms outstretched, trying to make the goal look smaller. Roy began his run-up, connected with the ball... I hoped, I prayed but it was all in vain as the ball hit the back of the net. GOAL – 1–0 Celtic. I sat back down with my head in my hands.

I daren't look at the Beach End. I didn't want to see the Celtic fans celebrate. Why should they be allowed to spoil our party, this wasn't how I imagined it all to be. I did look, but only for a few seconds or so as I felt sick to the stomach. Angus looked down at me, shrugged his shoulders, and looked at his watch. "Plenty of time to get back into the game – don't worry." I looked at my watch, he was quite right. Angus was always right in these situations and made me feel calmer, I trusted his judgement. Half-time was greeted with an eerie silence. The majority clapped both sides off the park but the nervousness very much in evidence before the game made an unexpected return during the 15-minute break. The hum of chit-chat was gone, replaced by a sense of quietness. The atmosphere made me uneasy. The only noise coming from inside the stadium was towards the Beach End as the Celtic fans enjoyed their slender lead. I tucked into my sausage roll while skimming through the matchday programme trying not to think the worst.

Celtic were first out after the break, soon followed by the Dons. I stood again, as did the whole of the Paddock, to greet our heroes and remind them we were still right behind them, despite the scoreline. Pat Bonner took his place in goal, either oblivious or doing his best to ignore the barrage of abuse he was receiving from those behind me. I watched Roy Aitken go round each of his players giving last-minute instructions; I quickly glanced at Willie Miller to see if he was doing the same – of course he was. Mark McGhee was pumping his fists, Neale Cooper stretching; Neil Simpson was jumping up and down in the centre of the park. Off we went again! It wasn't long before Pittodrie came alive again. The Dons received a free kick over on the right wing. All around me people stood up in anticipation. I watched Willie Miller and Alex McLeish move towards the Celtic penalty area. Ian Porteous stood over the ball. He delivered an outswinging cross. I watched the ball float over the Celtic 18-yard box. My eye caught Willie Miller. He was watching the ball – not a single Celtic player tracked his movement. I leaned a little higher on Angus's shoulder. I could see all that was about to unfold. Willie jumped, albeit a little awkwardly but, none-theless, somehow connected. I leant a little higher – now on my tip-toes. Packy Bonner dived full length but the ball was beyond his reach. Cue madness!

The net rippled. GOOOOOAAAALLLLLL!!!!! I screamed at the top of my lungs as Willie ran towards the South Stand celebrating a well deserved equaliser. I was jumping up and down while still attached to Angus's shoulder! The Paddock went berserk, as did the rest of Pittodrie. Folk all around me were congratulating each other, hugging. "We're going to win it now aren't we?" Angus nodded in agreement. For me, Willie scoring fitted the occasion. He was Aberdeen's leader, their finest player, and he and only he could write such a script. I was so excited, my first title. Kings of Scotland as well as Europe! The rest of the game was a blur. As full-time edged ever closer the whistles from behind me grew louder and louder, all begging for the referee to blow up – to bring the game to an end.

When that moment came it was met with another round of celebrations, very much like when Willie equalised. I was elated. The Paddock burst into song, "Championees, Championees are we are we are we!" This continued as the Dons players congratulated each other on the park. I looked over at Alex Ferguson who was as calm as I'd ever seen him. I was a tad disappointed to be honest; I was hoping for more of the comical sprint across the pitch, jumping all over his players but it wasn't to be. Age and experience obviously brought with it a sense of purpose but inside he must have been jumping through hoops (excuse the pun), maybe in his own private time he allowed himself a small celebration. We stayed long after the full-time whistle blew. By this time the Beach End was empty. We anticipated a return to the park from the victorious players; we didn't have to wait long. I stood high while cheering wildly. Here were my boys – champions of Scotland. Now I was in a position to fully comprehend what it meant. Aberdeen winning the league was a fantastic achievement; the Old Firm stranglehold on the league was well and truly over. There was a new kid on the block. There was a great sense of achievement around Pittodrie that day. Young and old together celebrated another marvellous milestone in the club's history. Looking back on all those years I feel privileged to have been part of it, albeit from the benches of the Paddock. I never tire of watching that game on DVD and allow myself a trip down memory lane to relive that glorious day. Now that I had a taste of it, I wanted more and expected the Dons to deliver.

Unfortunately, for thousands of Dons fans across the world that was the last time the Dons achieved success in the league. If I may be so bold to say, and with the greatest respect to current owner Stewart Milne who, in my opinion, with his fellow directors has done a marvellous job of keeping the business debt-free, unless the club finds a sugar daddy I doubt, in my lifetime, Aberdeen will ever win a title again. With the demise of Rangers and Hearts the best we can expect is to finish second. Celtic, with their superior fan base, superior wage structure, and Champions League revenue will dominate the game for years to come. I am not being pessimistic – I am being a realist. I understand on the day it's eleven versus eleven on the pitch and the application by the players ultimately determines the end result, but the Glasgow giants can attract technically more gifted players due to highly attractive contracts. How can we compete when the highest-paid player at Celtic earns up to £20,000 per week? And that's without bonuses!

The Dons did come close under the guidance of Alex Smith and Jocky Scott in 1990/91. In the very last game of the campaign, against Rangers at Ibrox, the Dons were pipped to the post. On the day I was playing in a cup final for Stoneywood Boys' Club under 17s, meaning I missed a large chunk of the game at Ibrox. I was able to put it to the back of my mind as another medal was added to the collection but as soon as we were done I showered quickly, ran to Dad's car, to find him slumped in his seat; "Losing 1–0," he said! We drove home listening to the game on the radio, praying the boys could find a path back into the game but it was obviously not meant to be as Rangers ran out winners and claimed another title. I was devastated! I'm not sure if the club actually recovered from that blow for the next few years.

The sacking of Alex Smith the next season, after some poor results, was premature but not unexpected and I was over the moon when Willie Miller was announced as the new Dons manager. I had every confidence Willie could turn the club's fortunes around and he so nearly did, finishing runners-up twice to Rangers in the league but unable to deliver the silverware the fans so desperately craved. When he was sacked I was gutted for him but not surprised. For the next few years Aberdeen fans clambered aboard a rollercoaster of football emotions. By this time my own life had taken a few twists and turns and my days at Pittodrie as a committed fan would come to an end. I have never been the same since!

Released

I had only just turned 16 and was facing my final year at Ellon Academy. I still had ambitions of becoming a professional footballer but those very same ambitions dwindled away after the biggest disappointment of my life – when I was told by Aberdeen Football Club that they would not offer me a professional contract. I remember the day like it was yesterday, it has stayed with me all my life and in some strange way I have used it as a means of reminding myself to stay strong throughout.

From a young age all I wanted to be was a pro and pull on the red and white of Aberdeen. I worked incredibly hard at my game, even though I was not exactly gifted or had the maturity to fully understand what it took to become a professional. It's not just about talent, a commanding attitude is required. Growing up, I played for a number of boys' clubs in the Aberdeen area. My first was Auchterellon Boys' Club, who I joined at the age of 12 after starting secondary school. For my first game I played in midfield with a young Derek Adams – former Aberdeen, Motherwell and Ross County midfielder and now manager of Ross County. Now take into consideration this was an under-13s side, Derek was only nine-years-old and already head and shoulders above the rest of us. Derek's father George refereed our game that cold Sunday morning and unbeknown to me at the time would go on to have a major influence on my teenage years.

George Adams is a legend in the game, very much like Eric Harrison at Manchester United in the early 1990s. Alongside his sidekick Lenny Taylor, George shaped the future of Aberdeen FC by coaching the crop of youngsters coming through the ranks. Having also worked at both Celtic and Rangers, George is now quite brilliantly guiding the fortunes of Ross County as their director of football. Playing on both a Saturday for a boys' club in a youth league in Aberdeen city, and Auchterellon in a county league on Sunday, George was able to cast his expert eye over me probably more than he could have wished for. On a Sunday I would pester him to watch me, to offer advice and invite me to training at Pittodrie where I hoped my dream would become a reality. Thinking back I probably drove the poor guy mad with my constant pecking!

As my game improved I was used by my boys' club managers in a number of different positions, be it centre-back, sweeper, midfield or even up front where my height and clumsy style of play maybe offered our opponents a headache or two. As I reached 14 I had settled as a defender and started to develop my game. I had been playing regularly every weekend for two seasons now and George was yet to invite me to training, I was getting frustrated but continued to work hard. At this time I was training almost every night. My only rest night was a Friday. Upon reaching 15 I became eligible to participate in the Scotland schoolboy trials. At school our head of PE Alan Dunbar selected a handful of boys to take part and thankfully my name was on the list. To cut a long story short the trials consisted of a number of games to be played out over a few months with teams being made up of boys from various districts and regions. The first trial I had to get through was for Grampian district, which was a game between all the top lads from a number of different schools in the county. Thankfully I made it through to the next stage.

From there I officially represented Grampian where we would face the best of the boys from the city of Aberdeen XI in the next trial match. This was a step up but having played against these lads most Saturday afternoons I knew what to expect. I raised my game and managed somehow to secure my passage to the next trial. Never at any point did I envisage that if I worked a bit harder and stayed mentally strong I could have made it all the way to represent Scotland. It still bugs me occasionally!

Next it was a trip into the Highlands of Scotland to face the best of the lads from the north and beyond. This was uncharted territory having never played against these lads before. I was picked to play at right-back and having only played a handful of games in that position I was nervous going into the game. Even for my standards back in 1988, I played a blinder but was injured in a clumsy challenge by some oaf who forced me off with an ankle knock! I believed my chance had passed me by and hid away on the sidelines under the subs' tracksuits cursing my luck. But for some reason, which I still think about now and then, lady-luck was obviously looking down on me that day as my coach, who was tending to my ankle, told me I had done enough to impress in the first half and I was definitely going through to the next round. I couldn't quite believe it but when all the names were called out after the game my name was second on the list! I was overjoyed and at the age of 15 was officially representing the North of Scotland Schoolboys XI. My Dad was particularly cock-a-hoop when I arrived home with my good news.

A month later, a trip down to Dundee to face the best of the boys from the Tayside region. I knew I would be facing lads who had already been snapped up by professional clubs so this was a big test for me. Unfortunately, my nerves got the better of me that day and by my own standards I had a very poor game. Not once did I venture forward to support my wingers as I was too afraid my immediate opponent would take advantage of this and I would be left woefully exposed at the back! I didn't play well at all and was not surprised to learn I had not done enough to make it through to Largs (Scotland's training base and education centre) where the best of the under-15 boys from Scotland met up to determine the final squad. I was devastated! I never said a word on the way home in the car back to Aberdeen – my Dad doing his best to lift my spirits.

On arriving home – just when I felt all was lost – Mum told me George Adams had been on the phone to see how I had got on in the trial and left a message for me to call him immediately. I didn't want to convey my bad news but Mum had a glint in her eye which gave me the confidence to ring him. George answered immediately and delivered a sentence which to this day I can remember like it was yesterday. He said; "Right, big man, I know you've had a disappointing day but I think it's about time we got you down to Pittodrie to start training." It took a second or two for those words to compute. I looked at Mum, she smiled brightly! I looked at Dad, he smiled brightly! George told me I would be picked up after school the following Tuesday by a club representative and driven to the ground. He said; "OK, big man?" I mumbled something on the lines of "thank you, see you Tuesday" and George hung up. That was that! A 30-second phone call which I believed would change my life!

Mum and Dad embraced me tightly and congratulated me. To be honest I was so shocked and confused that it felt almost surreal. What a weird day! I went to bed that night full of excitement and wonderment that at long last here was my big chance. The next couple of days went by in a flash and before I could take it all in here I was in a pokey, damp, dark room under the old Beach End stand at Pittodrie meeting the other lads who I all knew well. George and Lenny gathered us around and conveyed their instructions for what would be an extensive training session on the red ash car park directly across the road from the stadium. For those who are blissfully unaware of the skin-tearing pitches, red ash is a mixture of grit, sand and just about anything else that clings to the pre-historic surface! It's bloody awful and leaves a lasting mark when a sliding tackle is made in a game! I still squirm when thinking back at my poor Mum cleaning the grit out of my thighs with cotton wool and Dettol!

I trained with Aberdeen going on six months believing I was progressing well until a family holiday to Tenerife ended my dreams, aspirations and for a number of years my love of playing football. During our holiday to the Spanish isle I continued my training and worked with Dad most days – much to the annoyance of Mum who wanted us both to relax and enjoy the trappings of our favoured holiday destination. I couldn't wait to get back home and take up where I left off. I was not ready for what greeted me when I arrived at Pittodrie one cold October evening back in 1988, two days after our break. I trained as normal with the boys feeling assured and happy with my game that night. After changing and meeting Dad, George took me to one side and told Dad and I that he and Lenny Taylor had come to a difficult decision and delivered the type of news that in simple terms broke my heart forever! George told me I would not be invited back to training. I was stunned. He explained his reasons but those words were lost on me as I fought back the tears. Dad, by this time, held me close obviously feeling my pain and thanked

George for giving me the opportunity to train over the past few months. I cried all the way home and for the best part of the evening.

So at the age of 16 what did I learn from that setback? I needed to improve mentally and believe more in my game but I allowed nerves to dictate the most part of my teenage years. Looking back I should have been stronger but lacked the character to do so. This affected me for many years and I was never the same player again. George told me recently there were aspects of my game that needed improving – such as my positional awareness – but he believed with the time coaches get to develop players nowadays I may have fulfilled my early potential. I also confess with the power of hindsight I was not good enough. I know that now and should have realised it back then. I knew a career in the game was not meant to be so it was a case of dusting one's self down and getting on with it. I had no choice; I had my whole life in front of me. No point getting down on myself as much as the rejection pained me. We all have to face adversities in life but how we deal with it dictates the road we ultimately take. Be strong, look for the next opportunity and continue to believe in one's talent. George and I remain good friends to this day. He is a remarkable man. I hope to see him again very soon.

Destiny

Suppressing emotions during a football match has never been a particular strength of mine. At times my behaviour at a match mirrored that of a raving lunatic. From a young age I never shied away from singing the songs at the top of my voice, shouting and screaming at the players and losing all bodily control when Aberdeen scored a goal. It set the benchmark for my love and passion for the club. Even now, in my forties, the same passion is very much in evidence but I have mellowed somewhat. The Scottish League Cup is one such competition where all my emotions have come to the fore. Since 1981 I have only missed four cup finals Aberdeen have contested. Three of those have been in the League Cup. They have all been painful, but for many different reasons.

In season 1988/89, when the Dons made the semi-finals after a fairly straightforward passage past Arbroath, Morton and Hibs, Aberdeen's opponents before a potential day out at Hampden were Dundee United at Dens Park. Before school, when the announcement was made the game would be played at a neutral venue, Dad asked over breakfast if we should take another road trip as it had been a couple of years since we had all been at a game together as a family. Peter, in particular, was very excited as he had not been to a midweek game for a while, especially on a school night! I needed no persuading.

We decided the best option to make our way to Dundee. Peter, Mum and I would drive to the airport after school, meet Dad and then jump in Dad's car to make the two-hour drive south. An excellent plan, I thought. We arrived in plenty of time to take our place behind the goal at Dens Park. The atmosphere was building nicely and I expected nothing but a Dons win. Aberdeen showed their true class and grit as they ran out comfortable 2–0 winners, thanks to goals from Davie Dodds and John Hewitt. After impressive performances like we had just witnessed the drive home in the car always passed quicker, with only one topic of conversation dominating the two-hour journey – getting tickets for the cup final. Before I knew it I was tucked up in bed ready for school the next morning.

In the weeks leading up to the final, I kept pestering Dad to take us; I tried in vain to use some sort of emotional blackmail declaring that as a family we had to be there otherwise I feared the worst for the Dons. It was our duty to be there, we had a family tradition and we couldn't let the boys down by snubbing the game once again. I pleaded with him to do more to get four tickets; our very best efforts were required. Despite Dad's exertions, and those of others, we were unable to secure tickets for the final. This was a major blow so for the second successive year, as the Dons ran out at Hampden on October 23rd 1988 to face Rangers, the Begg family gathered in the living room of the family home in Newburgh to watch the game unfold on TV. I feared the worst! We had let the boys down.

All my pre-match fears and apprehensions slowly became reality as the game, which no doubt offered a marvellous advert for Scottish football, favoured Rangers. The Dons had put up a spirited fight, coming from behind twice, but it just wasn't meant to be. As I watched Terry Butcher lift the Skol Cup after a 3–2 win I couldn't help but feel it was our fault. We should have been there cheering the boys on, we were their lucky charm – or so I thought. I was devastated and told both Mum and Dad that I would not miss the Dons in a final again, come hell or high water! Here my story jumps 12 months in time. The same cup final, the same venue, and for the third successive year, the same opponents – Rangers! But unlike the past couple of years I walked over hot coals to be at the game. Nothing would stop me this time and as I took my place behind the goal with my pals I could not help but feel today, October 22nd, would be our day! I had made it to Hampden! I even allowed myself a moment of self-congratulation for going the extra yard to obtain my ticket.

In the early rounds the Dons had wielded the axe. Albion Rovers, Airdrie and St Mirren had been cast aside without any trouble. Celtic and the semi-finals awaited the Dons. As the game was on a Wednesday night at the national stadium a day-pass from school was not granted so an evening of comfort in one's own bedroom was my plan, BBC Radio Scotland my date! The Dons snatched victory from the jaws of defeat as Celtic had three strong penalty claims in the first half alone, all turned down by Brian McGinlay. It took a moment of brilliance from newly signed winger Ian Cameron, who had only joined the Dons two months earlier from St Mirren, to write himself into history and immediately become a Dons hero. His 25-yard screamer flew past Packy Bonner to spark wild scenes from those who had made the journey south. This time around, a herd of wild stampeding horses would not stop me from going to the final.

The very next day I phoned Angus and told him, no matter what, we had to go to the game. During our usual Sunday afternoon kick-about up on the links the lads and I decided to hire a minibus and hit the road to Glasgow. Tickets were obtained without too much bother and before I knew it I was sitting on the back seat with my rather tasty looking packed lunch ready to attend another final, the first without my family! The drive down the road was filled with much laughter, singing and piss-taking. As I was the youngest, most of the banter was aimed my way, not that I minded as I gave us good as I got! As we edged closer to Glasgow I started to feel nervous, the laughter was replaced by talk of the game and the team that Alex Smith would pick. If the Dons were to prevail, an unforgettable performance would have to be delivered over 90 minutes.

As we edged ever closer to Hampden, our bus was directed towards the convoy that had travelled from Aberdeen. Parked safely, we headed off to Hampden on foot. En route I stopped off to buy a flag, it was tradition after all. As we made our way into the stadium I felt a little sad that Mum, Dad and Peter were back home watching on from the relative comfort of the front living room. The last thing Dad said to me as we set off was to be careful and behave. I missed him on occasions like this. We took our place on the terraces behind the goal as the sun beat down on our heads; we had the perfect vantage point. The Red Army was in fine fettle as the songs rang out over the south side of Glasgow.

The Dons started the game brightly but at times rode their luck as Rangers hit the woodwork three times. Alex Smith and Jockey Scott had audaciously started with 18-year-old Eoin Jess in the centre of midfield; it was a masterstroke with the aging Ray Wilkins struggling to keep pace. When the Dons were awarded a free kick just outside the 18-yard box I hoped Jim Bett would just smash one in. Instead his shot was charged down but fell to the feet of Robert Connor, who dinked a ball into the box. At this point I noticed Rangers keeper Chris Woods leave his line but I sensed he wouldn't make it. My hunch proved correct as Paul Mason outjumped Stuart Munro and guided the ball over Woods's head into the back of the net.

Cue wild celebrations among the Newburgh boys, jumping up and down, Angus and I embracing each other screaming "yes, yes". I pictured Mum and Dad back home rejoicing. Maybe, just maybe, this would be our year. All around us Aberdeen fans sensed this could be our day, "stand free" and "here we go" sang to maximum volume. But, our joy soon turned to despair as referee George Smith made a howler to end all howlers when he inexplicably awarded Rangers a penalty not long after the Dons took the lead. A long ball was delivered up to Ally McCoist, he backed into Wille Miller, who did his best to avert the danger while McCoist went to ground. I shouted at the ref, "C'mon ref, he can't back in like that." My plea was lost in the deafening roar that greeted my ears far to my right, the Rangers fans were jumping up and down in celebration. What were they doing?

As my eyes met the scene I could not quite believe what I was looking at! Smith had pointed to the spot and awarded Rangers a penalty. I held my head in my hands. Around me Aberdeen fans were screaming, swearing, looking for reason. A red pack formed round Smith as the Dons players argued their case; Smith in turn booked big Alex McLeish for dissent! There was plenty more dissent heading his way from the terraces behind the goal, believe me! It was an appalling decision and the arguments continued as Mo Johnston smugly tucked away the penalty. Thankfully, the Dons kept their wits about them and continued to ride the storm as Rangers took a foothold in the game. As the second half came and went Theo Snelders, in particular, was in astounding form as extra time loomed!

When the final whistle pierced the Glasgow sky I started to believe we could do this. I always fancied us during the extra period, plus the omen of never having seen the Dons lose in the extra period meant we had the edge; it was my omen and I believed there and then we would go on and win the cup and lay the ghost of the two previous years to rest. Here we go! Willem Van Der Ark was introduced to the fray and gave the Dons a different attacking option – the long ball! With only a few minutes of the first period remaining the Dons won a throw in the far left-hand corner. David Robertson prepared to launch one of his missiles into the box. Big Willem placed himself between Terry Butcher and Richard Gough; he easily outjumped the two of them to get the faintest of touches. As this happened I grabbed Angus by the arm. I had not done this in years. I sensed something!

My eyes opened wider as Charlie Nicholas controlled the ball superbly, laid it off and… GOOOOOOAAALLLL!!!!! Paul Mason smashed a low drive into the bottom of the net, which left Chris Woods stranded. I leapt up and down, using Angus as a lever. I was screaming, "yes, yes, yes". All around me strangers were grabbing each other, enjoying the moment together. I continued to scream at the top of my voice, grabbing Angus and the others as we celebrated together. I was delirious, on the verge of madness! I had wanted this so much and the goal had offered me a moment to lose control of myself.

The half-time whistle blew and the teams changed ends. I watched Terry Butcher try to rally his troops but I sensed defeat was in the air for the men in blue. Rangers were done; all we had to do was hold on for another 15 minutes. This was done with ease as the full-time whistle was met with a roar that would have ignited the Northern Lights. The Aberdeen end was rocking; it was a wonderful spectacle watching all the different faces enjoying the Dons winning a cup. I was overcome with joy. In fact, I think I was on the verge of tears.

This win meant so much; the Dons were still a force to be reckoned with. As Willie Miller lifted the Skol Cup high into the late afternoon air it was met with a cheer I doubt I will hear again. I stood and put my arms in the air, grinning from ear to ear. I loved this moment. I knew deep down I had gone the extra mile to be at Hampden that day; I convinced myself I was the reason behind the Dons' success. I vowed there and then I would never miss another final. My record was safe!

The drive home was a laugh-a-minute as we sang our hearts out. Scarves and flags hung from every window as we relived what was a famous victory against all the odds. The banter flowed, the beer flowed and before I knew it we were turning off the A94 and heading the final couple of miles into the village. I couldn't wait to get home and tell Mum and Dad about my day. We dropped the lads off one by one, all offering a final hug and a congratulatory pat on the back for a trip well worth the effort. When I walked through the front door I was met by Dad, who grabbed me and hugged me tight. "What a great day," I whispered in his ear, "I wish you could have been there." He smiled at me, put his arm round my shoulder and led me into the kitchen where he clicked on the kettle, took my jacket, sat me down and said; "Come on then, tell me all about it."

Hampden in the sun

The 1990 Scottish Cup Final against Celtic will go down in history. For the first time ever; the competition had to be settled by penalty kicks. For anybody in attendance that day, the tension bordered on the unbearable! For 120 minutes nothing could separate two sides, determined to cancel each other out. En route to the final, Aberdeen knocked out Partick Thistle, Morton and Hearts, scoring 12 goals on the way. Dundee United stood between us and another date at Hampden. An impressive 4–0 victory meant the Dons would contest a Scottish Cup Final for the first time in four years. In the weeks leading up to the game, I felt a burning desire to go. I was 17 and finding my way in the world. I had a good job at the old Bon Accord Baths working as a trainee lifeguard, earning my own money, clubbing on a regular basis and using Mum and Dad's house as a means of convenience. As the weeks became days, I had still not managed to secure a ticket and a mild panic started to set in. I also had another small problem to deal with, my boys' club game scheduled for the same day.

I honestly felt a sense of hopelessness as the game edged ever closer, I even considered "borrowing" Dad's car for the day, driving down to Glasgow and trying to find a tout. On the Wednesday before the game my luck suddenly changed. During a shift at work I received a message to call my Dad immediately, which I promptly did. He told me to get down to the Rosemount Bar where the landlord had a ticket for me! I made my excuses for an early lunch, jumped on the bus and headed off. At first I thought it was a cruel wind-up but low and behold the ticket was there. Up until then, it was one of the best moments of my life! I paid for the ticket and headed back to work, feeling full of the joys of life. Now that I had a ticket, there was just one more hurdle to get over, my boys' club game. Fate most definitely played its lucky hand that day as my match was cancelled for reasons I still don't know to this day. So, a lovely spring day on May 12th 1990 and I took my place among the Dons fans on the terracing behind the goal at Hampden Park.

In regulation time, there was nothing really to shout home about but like all Dons fans on the day, we thanked God for Theo Snelders. The big Dutch goalkeeper pulled off a couple of remarkable saves to keep us in the contest. At the end of extra time, penalties beckoned. I felt a huge sense of trepidation as historically Aberdeen did not exactly cover themselves in glory when it came to holding their nerve in a shoot-out. All around me Dons fans were shaking their heads and quietly discussing what might happen.

I remember one lad turning round to me and saying, "I don't think I can watch." He wasn't the only one! I know it's an old cliché but you could honestly have cut the atmosphere with a knife. As the first five penalties were converted, the tension grew as sudden death approached. However, even in the midst of such pressure, I discovered a new-found respect for Charlie Nicholas who had to step up to the plate for the Dons knowing he would be re-joining his boyhood heroes at Parkhead in the close season. His penalty was first class.

So, on we went. A further three penalties were converted by the Dons and then it was the turn of Celtic full-back Anton Rogan. Years after the event, when I first started working for Setanta, I was looking through some old tapes from the vast library at Scottish Television for a feature I was co-producing for Celtic TV and happened to stumble across the footage of the penalty shoot-out. As Anton Rogan begins the long walk to the penalty box the television pictures cut to a wee Celtic fan, no more than 12-years-old, and he can clearly be seen mouthing; "Oh no, not Rogan!" Did that young lad have a sixth sense – maybe he did! To be fair to Rogan, he could not have struck the ball any better but the remarkable agility of Snelders meant he was able to dive full length to his left to tip the ball round the post. The Aberdeen end erupted. All around me Dons fans were jumping up and down in sheer excitement, complete strangers hugging each other, folk of all ages were delirious. I could see Theo Snelders screaming with joy, enjoying his own special moment, sharing it with the fans behind the goal.

But, there was still a job to do, the scores stood at 8-8 with advantage to the Dons! Score the next penalty and we would celebrate another Scottish Cup triumph. Up stepped Brian Irvine. All around me a hush descended among the fans, people were holding their hands to their mouths, some in prayer, some even looking away. I can't really explain how I was feeling but my stomach was turning over; I think I even looked to the heavens at one point. My nerves were in turmoil and I was physically shaking. Brian stepped up and fired the ball high into the net, sending Pat Bonner the wrong way. What a moment as the Aberdeen end exploded; it was pandemonium as fans of all ages celebrated with each other; some overcome with emotion, some not able to comprehend what had just happened. I just jumped up and down for five minutes!

I always wondered what went through Brian's mind as he stepped up to take the penalty. He told me recently he didn't feel as nervous as he thought he would, as he knew if he missed – unlike the other lads who HAD to score – the Dons were still in with a chance. All the pressure would then fall back again on Theo to save the next penalty! He went on to say that it was a fantastic moment, and a great feeling knowing he had achieved something of lasting value for the club.

Brian also told me there was great excitement in the dressing room long after the last kick as the adrenaline still pumped through the players. He also admitted that it takes a long time to come back to earth after a Scottish Cup Final, as it is usually the last match of the season!

Tasting defeat

By the time the 1992 League Cup Final came around, I had been living and working in London for just over 12 months. Things were good. I had just been offered the opportunity of a lifetime with Bad Boys Inc, but those crazy days were still very much in their infancy. My modelling career had taken a turn for the better when renowned modelling agency Models 1 took me on as a client and my workload doubled almost overnight. I was happy and content for the first time since making the bold move to the English capital.

I had recently started playing football again. My agency Models 1 did not exactly encourage this out-of-school activity for fear of serious injury but I missed playing and wanted the buzz again. Not long after moving to London my Sunday mornings were spent travelling all over the city playing for Heathrow Airport FC!! I had discovered a void in my life, not going to Pittodrie on a regular basis felt alien and I missed it. I missed the company of my friends and family, I missed the atmosphere, the fans, the colour, the players, the Bovril and occasional sausage roll! Playing again helped fill a small part but it certainly wasn't a substitute!

I kept up to speed with the Dons via the usual methods in 1992, Teletext, Final Score on *Grandstand*, or via the radio. As Saturday was my usual day off, it meant a day in my studio apartment on Chiswick High Road listening intently for any match report. The league campaign had started well and the Dons were playing an attractive brand of football. Willie Miller's chosen style seemed to suit his players and I had high hopes of a successful season. The League Cup campaign started with a comfortable away win against Arbroath but the next round against Dunfermline proved a difficult nut to crack, only an extra-time winner by Mixu Paatelainen saving the Dons' blushes.

The Bairns of Falkirk were disposed of in the quarters, the Dons winning 4–1, but then came the big test; Liam Brady's Celtic in the semis at Hampden. I toyed with the idea of going up to Glasgow for the game but as skint as I was back then, it was a pipe-dream. Under Brady, the Hoops had struggled but still had a team full of great players. Tom Boyd, Paul McStay, John Collins, to name but a few. The rain made for a dreary night at Hampden but over 40,000 fans still turned up for what would be a closely fought encounter with the only goal of the game coming just before half-time, thanks to a fine finish from Eoin Jess.

Celtic only started playing in the final ten minutes and came close to an equaliser after Gerry Creaney hit the bar with a header, but the Dons held on and another Skol Cup Final beckoned! After the 1989 success I was not going to miss this for the world! As soon as the full-time whistle blew, I did my usual comical celebration – on my own I hasten to add – then called my Dad and the decision was taken that another family day out at the grand old stadium was on the cards! I only had to wait a month! At that time, Dad owned a small aviation company operating out of Aberdeen Airport and was able to book me on a staff ticket via British Airways. I flew up from Heathrow to Glasgow and met up with the family. I looked forward to our day out immensely as it was going on six years since we had all been together for a cup final. October 25th was a day just like any other in the south side of Glasgow, cloudy and cold as Aberdeen faced Rangers yet again!

The 1992 Skol Cup Final was the fourth time this pairing had contested the final in six years. We took our seats in the main stand near the back and settled down to watch the game. We sat amongst a few Dandies but as was the norm in the old stand, we could not escape the company of Rangers fans, two of whom were stewards manning the exit. These two clowns, for all the wrong reasons, would leave a lasting impression. Rangers had stamped their authority on the Scottish game and were the dominant force with a team full of international stars, from both sides of the border, so my nerves were a little fraught!

The Dons started the game well but it was Rangers who took the lead thanks to a Stuart McCall goal. As I held my head in my hands, I was aware of one of the stewards celebrating. I did my best to ignore the inappropriate behaviour but it was virtually impossible not to be annoyed by it! As the game ebbed and flowed, the Dons midfield of Eoin Jess, Brian Grant, Jim Bett and Roy Aitken started to get a foothold on the game. Rangers went into the half-time break a goal to the good but I still felt confident we could get back into it. Peter and I disappeared downstairs to get some refreshments but as we did the stewards started making derogatory comments about Aberdeen fans. Again, I was a little perturbed but simply raised a smile at the guy and shook my head. As the second half kicked off, I was still feeling confident we could snatch an equaliser and my sixth sense proved accurate as Duncan Shearer turned superbly to fire a well-placed shot past Andy Goram.

Well, my brother Peter and I needed no invitation. Leaping out our seats we celebrated together while the steward looked on in disgust. He made his way back to his post. My confidence grew as the game made its way into extra time. The

Dons were playing well, creating chances and matching Rangers on all fronts. But then the unimaginable happened. Just as the Dons were getting on top, Aberdeen defender Gary Smith diverted the ball past Theo Snelders for an own goal as he tried to cut out a cross.

I couldn't believe it and it took a few seconds for my brain to compute what had just happened. I looked over at my Dad and even though I was 20-years-old, and had played the game to a fairly decent standard, I still needed his reassurance everything was going to be OK. Unfortunately, he was just as dumbfounded; Peter held his head in his hands! It was a horrible moment and I knew we were going to lose. I did my best to ignore the two stewards celebrating wildly beside us but their behaviour grated. The rest of the game went by in a blur. When the full-time whistle blew I needed no invitation to get out of there. As we made our exit the stewards continued to celebrate and mock a few Aberdeen fans as they left. Their inappropriate behaviour was not becoming of our beloved sport and sportsmanship in my opinion should always be observed at any level. There is a time and a place to celebrate. The safety of those leaving the stadium should have been high on their priority list, not mocking emotional fans of opposing teams. Poor show by those who are, after all, employed for our safety! The journey back to Bishopbriggs was a long and quiet one. Defeat hurt and I felt sick to the stomach. I just wanted to get back to London as soon as possible and forget about the game. I duly jumped on the early morning flight from Glasgow and put it to the back of my mind. I had to wait three more years for my next cup final. Like this one, it will always be etched in my memory, but for completely different reasons.

Bad Boys Inc

In November 1992, I was offered the opportunity to embark on a life-changing journey. The journey and subsequent experience had a huge bearing on my life; it changed me from a person I knew, to a person I did not. Twenty years later I am still questioning one's reasoning behind the whole charade! In this chapter I am going to try and delve deep into the minds of fans, be it those of football or boy bands. I am not pretentious enough to presume that you, the reader of this book, are aware that between the years 1992 and 1995 I was a member of a relatively successful boy band called Bad Boys Inc. Well, I was and as they say – the rest is history!

I do, now, many years later, feel quite blessed to have participated in such an incredible experience but it took many years of soul-searching, questioning one's sanity and reasoning to be totally comfortable with what I did. For a very long time I distanced myself from the band and anything to do with it. The experience weighed down on me and engulfed me for the first few years after we went our separate ways. I couldn't escape it, even when I wanted to. I do not hold any grudges anymore, but for a number of years I allowed my weaknesses to dictate my anger and frustration at the very people who I believed were there to look after us. Thankfully, now I couldn't give a flying shit!

This may come as a surprise to many people as surely the perception of being a pop star is fame, money, girls, glamour, talent, bling, luxury etc etc etc – trust me it is NOT! You're probably wondering at this point what I'm complaining about as so many clamber to taste what I experienced all those years ago. I am not trying to sound ungrateful or dismissive but I am trying to get across the point that it's not actually all that it's cracked up to be. This brings me to the point of this chapter; I never really understood the fascination. What makes a fan a fan? Why choose us instead of boy bands who, in my opinion, were so much more successful than us, better looking than us, and maybe more talented than us?

Why do girls, and the odd gay man it has to be said, scream at the top of their lungs at the very sight of pop stars? Why do girls shake uncontrollably, faint or come across all silly when in direct contact with just another human being? A human being who, let's face it, they don't really know that well, a human being who has been presented as an image but, at the end of the day, is just another human being! Why do they camp outside houses and spend fortunes following their "boys" up and down the country? I always struggled to understand; even today as I pen this book I still don't really get it! I will elaborate on this later but I was plucked from obscurity, placed in a very weird position very quickly, without comprehending what was happening, and made to feel the adulation was just part of the job without fully realising, or understanding, it. I was brainwashed into thinking the adulation was deserved!

What I have discovered is a pattern. I can only speak for myself, and my opinions may differ from my boy band colleagues, but in the early days I loved the attention. It was so very exciting. Having girls scream at you and idolise you is everything any guy wants, right? I will never forget stepping out of HMV on Oxford Street in central London after a record signing and being faced by a wall of screaming faces. Office workers hanging out their windows as far as the eye could see, with police helicopters flying above. The police quickly ushered us into our waiting car and escorted us to safety. Meanwhile, the lads and I were doing our own version of screaming in the back of the car!

Once in Newcastle, at an open-air concert, the fans stormed the stage and we had to crawl on our hands and knees through the legs of security guards to escape. These poor unfortunate souls, having to hold back 10,000 screaming girls while we clambered into the car falling over the top of each other. Unbelievable scenes that I can still picture today! Then it was fun, it was novel and I liked it, but the novelty soon wore off as the months turned into years. After eight months or so when the exhaustion was really kicking in, the attention was wearing thin. I still enjoyed it to a degree but the honeymoon period was well and truly over. The adulation had become part of the job. Don't get me wrong, I still felt very flattered, and maybe a touch humbled, by it but I was becoming confused. Why on a daily basis were girls who had never met me before telling me they loved me – they didn't love me at all! The fans were in love with a fantasy, an image they hoped one day would offer them something more. It's not just in the pop world this exists; the whole of society is obsessed with fantasy. Whether we like it or not, we live in a celebrity-obsessed world. We have allowed our lives to be dictated by celebrity. Who is shagging who, who has done this, or who has done that? It makes me so very grateful that I grew up when I did!

The beginning of the end for me was when the adulation became my poison. I just didn't get it anymore, what was the fascination? I so desperately wanted to be left alone; I didn't want people staring at me anymore, or bothering me when I went to a football match. I tried so hard to do "my job" and accommodate the fans, I felt it was my duty but the constant need to bow down to their needs was overbearing at times. What I really struggled with is the fact that, relatively speaking, we were not really that successful if you compare us with the likes of New Kids on the Block, Take That, East 17 and boy bands of my era, so why the constant attention? Maybe because these guys had become so successful they became untouchable, impenetrable or maybe just too big for their own good. Maybe we were easy pickings because we were accessible to the fans, or the industry didn't take us seriously? I wish I knew, but no matter what, the craziness continued right up until the day we went our separate ways! Where I do take solace from the fans – and I only discovered this recently while lost in my own thoughts one night – is the fact that 20 years on they have remained incredibly loyal!

Twitter and Facebook pages have been set up. Friendships among the fans, which were formed in the early days, have remained strong to this day. Fans who followed us in the early days are now married and have children of their own yet still take the time to send messages and take a genuine interest in the fortunes of David, Tony, Matthew and I. You can almost argue their lives have evolved just as much as ours. The bond is strong and it's humbling! It's obvious to me now – but not back then – that they had a great time. They loved our music and maybe, just maybe, we became a catalyst for them as much as they became a catalyst for us!

Are football fans in the same mould? Do they behave the same way when faced with meeting their heroes up close and personal? Footballers, whether they like it or not, are like pop stars. The marketing monster engulfing the game dictates top players almost have no choice but to adhere to the rules. Yes, they receive many perks and get paid handsomely for their time, but are they really an equivalent to a Robbie Williams, Justin Bieber or the One Directions of this world? For me, the "fame game" is all so very unnecessary. I was always very uncomfortable with being perceived as a "celebrity". I know this may come as a surprise to some, considering my line of work and the privileged position it put me in, but as far as I was concerned being in a boy band or presenting on TV was nothing more than a job. It just so happened my job put me in the glare of the public eye.

Now that I have left my television-presenting career behind to work behind the cameras, I have never felt more comfortable with myself than I have since I was 18-years-old. I should have given up years ago to concentrate on a career in production. Many of my friends over the years have asked me what it was really like to be a member of Bad Boys Inc. I confess it's only been over the past few years that I have been able to talk openly about my experiences. After we split up, I did not talk about the band for years. If quizzed, I would change the subject or offer my apologies and say I didn't want to talk about it. The split, and the subsequent treatment from people, whom I understood were there to look after us, left a very bitter taste in my mouth.

I was left perplexed, confused, agitated and let down. Nobody seemed to care that four young lads, who were all in their early twenties, had been left in such dire straits, both financially and psychologically. I bore a grudge for many years. The phone stopped ringing, the hangers-on moved on, and people didn't need an excuse to "have a go". I knew a thick skin would be required to deal with the aftermath, but for me, I not only developed a thick skin but I built a brick wall around me just to make sure I could cope. I dealt with the situation on my own but my Mum and my late Dad were an incredible source of strength, offering financial help as well as encouragement to seek an alternative career. My Dad's business experience, and the help of David's father, helped dig the band out of a very deep hole. I thank God they stepped in and took over!

We travelled the world, met some incredible people, and performed in front of royalty at the Children's Royal Variety Show at the London Palladium. But, that does not disguise the fact it was incredibly hard work and, at times, soul-destroying. I am proud of what we achieved yet I honestly believe we could have achieved much more given the opportunity to experiment with different sounds and work with modern producers. When this was presented to us, mainly thanks to the hard work done behind the scenes at A&M Records, the end result was astonishing. Matthew travelled to New York to record a track with renowned music producer Rick Wakeman. Upon hearing the track for the first time I was covered in goose bumps. Could this be our ticket to unparalleled success? The simple answer to that question was NO as the collaboration never came to fruition. It was such a shame that our producer's ego stopped us from ultimately becoming more successful. Correct me if I am wrong, but wasn't that the objective in the first place?

So, with that all said and done, allow me to tell you the story of Bad Boys Inc to fully understand where I am going with this chapter. First of all, there has always been confusion regarding how we came to be. We were manufactured just like many others so up until the day we officially formed I had never met Tony Dowding, David Ross or Matthew Pateman. To cut a very long and laborious story short, in November 1992 I was asked to attend a record producer's recording studios in Chiswick, west London to meet with a gentleman who had seen one of my modelling photographs. I made my way to his studios keeping a very open mind! As I stepped into the pokey studio, I was asked to take a seat upstairs and told someone would be with me shortly. I could not help but

notice a number of awards displayed on the walls. I have
to say I was fairly impressed. By now I was starting to get
very intrigued! After what seemed like an age, a gentleman
appeared and introduced himself as "the producer". I was
shocked at his appearance; he was huge and obviously partial
to the finer things in life. The audition went something like
this:

Over the next half an hour he proceeded to tell me what
his vision was and where he saw me fitting in. He already had
a name for the band, "Bad Boys Inc" and an album was in
place to be recorded. I confessed immediately that I could not
sing and was probably tone deaf; he told me not to worry as
singing lessons were all part of the deal. After chatting for a
short while about the music industry, management companies,
PR people and photographers etc, he asked me to take my top
off!! I asked him why, and he told me he wanted to see if my
body would be appealing enough for young girls. I burst out
laughing at his request but did what he asked. He then asked
me to dance! Now, I really was wondering what his motives
were. He put on some music and I busted some moves for
him, offering the odd hip gyration along the way. I had to
disguise the fact that I was doubled up laughing for the most
part. "The producer" told me he was very happy and offered
me the job. End of audition!

Tony Dowding, a model and male stripper, soon became the
second member of the band. Tony, with his blonde hair and
washboard stomach, would break many a heart! Not long after,
a young actor/model by the name of David Ross joined. David
originated from Bournemouth and I warmed to him immediately with his wicked sense of humour a real selling point! A few
weeks passed by when "the producer" called me round to the
studio straight away, in his words he had found "a gift from

God". Matthew Pateman was indeed a gift from the heavens and after singing a rendition of George Michael's "Careless Whisper" he was hired as our lead singer! This 22-year-old from Bromley, south London had the most incredible voice. Thank Christ he did as his dress sense left much to be desired. He fitted in perfectly and I warmed to him from the off. Bad Boys Inc was complete!

After the final line-up was officially announced to the media, "the producer" asked 1st Avenue Management to manage us. Two very successful music industry moguls, Oliver Smallman and Denis Ingoldsby, owned the company. Between them, they had brokered many artists and boasted numerous hit records. I was thrilled they were going to guide our careers but, unfortunately, my elation soon turned to despair. Still, not long after we signed to 1st Avenue, A&M records came calling and in May 1993, Bad Boys Inc signed a five-album record deal. For this agreement, we each received an advance of £6,000, a paltry sum considering how much everybody else was earning from the deal. From here on in, my life changed dramatically. I had to give up the day job. Singing lessons, dance rehearsals, photoshoots, interviews and recording became part of the norm. I was now a fully paid-up member of the exclusive "pop star" club! That's when I knew my life would never be the same again.

After the record deal was signed, sealed and delivered, there was a real buzz in the band. It appeared everybody and their dog wanted a piece of us. The hype surrounding the band almost bordered on the ridiculous and we hadn't even released our first single. Bad Boys Inc was the first band to appear on the front cover of *Smash Hits* magazine without fully finalising a record deal.

It was all terribly exciting but the hard work crept up on us unsuspectingly. We, as a newly formed boy band, set off on a nationwide tour. As was par for the course for boy bands in the early 1990s, we embarked on a nationwide tour of under- and over-18 nightclubs in an attempt to build a fanbase. With the benefit of hindsight, the schedule was far too extensive; it was not unusual for us to perform five/six times a night, starting in an under-18 club in the early evening, before finishing at an over-18 venue in the small hours. In the very early days, we only performed one or two songs, but as time went on our set soon changed to half a dozen or more. As well as touring, we had interviews to conduct with magazines, newspapers, radio stations and TV.

Our schedule was exhausting but very rewarding. The gigs were going well and the singing lessons were starting to pay off as my voice started to develop. The choreography was also coming together nicely and our set was looking very polished and professional. After what seemed like an eternity, the release date for our first single "Don't Talk About Love" was set for August 23rd 1993. Not long after we arrived back from Majorca, where we made our first music video, we were told the very exciting news that Radio One wanted us to be their warm-up act on the famous Radio One Road Show. This was a huge thrill and a very important step in our short career. The tour itself lasted three weeks and we took in Northern Ireland, the north of England and Scotland, including Aberdeen. Up until we left for Scotland, the tour was going incredibly well and we were being well received by all.

The Aberdeen gig on July 14th 1993 was especially memorable as it was my first opportunity to perform in front of my friends and family. The lads stayed up in the Tree Tops Hotel but I made the decision to stay at home with Mum, Dad and Peter in Newburgh. When we arrived at the hotel it was swarming with fans and as we stepped off the tour bus, a crush ensued. I was concerned, not only for our own safety, but that of the fans who had turned up to see us and it took a wee while to eventually make it into the relative calm of the hotel. I had pre-arranged with Dad to meet me at the back of the building, by the tradesmen's entrance, so we could make a swift exit and head home.

It was the first time in a number of days that I felt normal again as Dad and I chatted all things "pop-star". Upon our arrival in the village, I was stunned to see a number of fans camped outside the house, as well as some photographers and members of the press. I spent a good hour outside with everybody before even greeting Mum or Peter; it was all very surreal! It was also the best night's sleep I'd had in ages. I think the comforts of home helped me relax and take my mind off the madness that was going on in my life at that time. The gig itself was a blur. Thousands of fans had gathered on the links by the beach just behind Pittodrie. It took an age to get into the compound, and the noise that greeted our arrival was deafening.

The actual performance itself went by quickly. I could hardly hear myself, or the track for that matter, as the levels of screaming hit new levels. I recall seeing my family and friends gathered at the back of the crowd, watching on in what seemed like a state of bemusement and bewilderment! Possibly, many of them found it difficult to actually believe that a normal lad from Newburgh was now performing in front of thousands of screaming fans on the Radio One Road Show! To be honest, the feeling was mutual. Unbeknown to me at the time an old school friend was recording the gig and he recently posted the performance on YouTube. Looking back all those years ago I cringe at what went on. I have no recollection of dropping my trousers, or lifting my shirt to bare my torso to the screaming fans. I wish I hadn't but the only excuse I can offer is I was caught up in the moment!

What I do vividly remember about the day was not the gig, or the fans, or the adulation, but an unscheduled trip to Pittodrie. After the performance a journalist from the *Sunday Mail* approached me and asked if I would be interested in doing an interview and photoshoot with Aberdeen legend Willie Miller. I didn't have to think too long to accept his offer. So the next thing I know, I'm standing in the middle of Pittodrie kicking a ball about with Tony feeling a tad apprehensive about meeting one of my schoolboy heroes.

Only 20 minutes before I had been over on the Beach Links with fans screaming at me, finding it all rather strange, yet exhilarating. Now the roles have been completely reversed and I found myself in the role of "fan". I had met Willie before as a youngster outside Hampden and asked him for his autograph but never felt the need to scream in his face or have heart palpitations in his presence! He came over with his assistant manager at the time, Roy Aitken, a player as a child I detested. I immediately felt nothing but shame for hating this man as a professional football player; it's what we do as youngsters and fans. We have our own pantomime villain. It's all part of football, it's part of the make-up of the game. For the record, Roy is one of the loveliest guys I have ever met. I hope our paths cross sometime soon again.

Willie introduced himself – as if he needed to – and firmly took my hand, as did Roy. I said hello and thanked them both for their time. As the photographer was clearly in a rush he put us in place and took the obligatory shots. I had other things on my mind; I desperately wanted to have a kick-about with Willie. Almost sheepishly, I asked him if we could and he duly obliged. Here was my childhood hero playing football with me, on the pitch at Pittodrie. I was living the dream, it was unbelievable and I did my best to show him I could play a bit! I was overwhelmed with joy, but not starstruck.

I kept my emotions in touch but loved every minute of it. This is where my confusion lies, why are some fans incapable of keeping their own emotions under control when faced with their heroes? Maybe it's a personality trait? Maybe it's weakness? Maybe it's lust? Or could it be as simple as a case of fascination? What I do know is that morning at Pittodrie is one of my fondest memories of that period with the band. As I mentioned at the beginning of the book, I have been extremely fortunate to meet the odd celeb along the way but to me they are just ordinary people working away like everyone else trying to earn their crust. But, I did once – I confess – make a complete tool of myself in front of comedian Billy Connolly!

During my time with Setanta and Celtic TV, I was fortunate to meet some rather interesting and colourful characters. Outside of football, there are people who I admire and respect, and Billy is very high up on the list. Billy, as most know, is a huge Celtic fan so imagine my delight when I found myself staring at the "Big Yin" ahead of Paul Lambert's testimonial dinner in Glasgow. He had been asked by Paul to host the evening. That same night, I was booked to go down to the venue to try and obtain a number of interviews for the following day's *Daily Huddle*. Ian, our cameraman, set up his equipment in a corner of the vast room out of harm's way as I manoeuvred through the crowd looking for suitable interviewees. During a break I asked Ian if he thought I should pop over and ask Billy if he would offer us a few words, but was reluctant to do so as he had given Celtic TV a lengthy interview only a week or two prior to Paul's dinner. Ian persuaded me to go over, chuckling at my obvious nervousness.

As I approached Billy I started to come over all silly. Here was the man who, from a very young age, I had watched on video time and time again and howled with laughter to the point where it was too sore to continue watching. Here was a man who helped develop my own inadmissible use of bad language, the man who is responsible for my own style of storytelling and humour. Here was the man whose TV show *Billy Connolly's World Tour of Scotland* gave my Dad the inspiration to start his own tourism business when he decided to call it a day in aviation. As I approached feeling very awkward, Billy was in deep conversation with a gentleman called Russell Kyle, who once managed Billy many moons ago and is now one half of a very successful PR agency in Scotland called PMPR.

I decided to step in and without speaking offered Billy my hand, which he did not take. Instead he crossed his arms over his chest, which simply added to my already uncomfortable mood. I looked him in the eye and introduced myself, explaining who I was and what I was doing. As soon as I mentioned "presenter of Celtic TV", his persona changed immediately. He said, "Ah! Hello son," took my hand firmly and shook it. I asked him sheepishly if he could spare me two minutes to offer a word or two about Paul Lambert. He unfortunately declined and this is where my world fell apart as for the next 30 seconds I made a complete fool of myself – not for the first time in my life I hasten to add – but the first time I have actively made myself look like a complete and utter tit in front of a celebrity!

Only two weeks prior to that evening, Billy had sat down in Stirling ahead of his stand-up show with our reporter Margot McCuaig to talk about his one true love in life, Celtic Football Club. Margot interviewed Billy for over an hour and it made for brilliant viewing. Billy explained to me that he had only recently sat down with Celtic TV and was not in the mood to do anything additional. Now, please take into consideration Margot was, at that time, my producer. I would like to think that I knew her fairly well. I said to Billy; "Yes I completely understand as you spoke to…" Suddenly, my mind went a complete blank but, unfortunately, I carried on talking. "Yes, Billy, you spoke to our reporter… erm… eh…" I could not for the life of me remember Margot's name!

However, instead of stopping, I continued, now sweating and feeling a tad stupid. "Erm, yes, you spoke to… erm." I could picture Margot but I could not find her name! I looked up and could see exactly what Billy was thinking without actually saying it; "For fuck's sake son, spit it out." Margot's name refused to come, my brain had slipped out of gear, and my coolness had gone! My stomach turned over. I stuttered, stammered but tried to smile at the same time. I was mortified and quickly gave up. I offered my humble apologies, wished both Billy and Russell a pleasant evening and sheepishly made my way back to our camera position.

As Ian sensed something was up I relayed the story to him at which point he needed to sit down in fear of falling over for laughter. Mr Connolly would continue to play a very small role during my time at Celtic TV. On my last *Daily Huddle* before making the move to Singapore, the production team surprised me with a small message from Billy who pretended that I was a long lost friend, even though he had no idea who I was and kidded on to wish me a fond farewell. The short message was hilarious as he told me not to eat chewing gum in Singapore, as my ass would be in jail before I knew what was happening! That 30-second clip from Billy is one of the highlights of my life; I only wish Dad had been alive to have seen it too as he was also a huge Billy Connolly fan.

So, why did I come across all silly while in the company of

Billy but not in the company of Willie Miller? I have tried to work this out and wonder if the level of celebrity differs. Are football players actual celebrities? I suggest over the years players who have taken on this mantle are few and far between but their level of fame indirectly has made them celebrities to you and I. George Best, Pele, David Beckham, Lionel Messi and Ronaldo, to name but a few. To me, these guys are nothing but professional football players. Yes, George Best started it, and David Beckham has taken it to new levels, but I have met both and wasn't overly bothered by meeting them. It was very nice and I enjoyed their company but I was not for one moment starstruck. I was able, with both, to engage in conversation quite normally without getting tongue-tied or nervous. Could it be that because I played the game I felt common ground?

David is an exception to the rule. He is an astonishingly handsome man and I have witnessed at close quarters both males and females completely lose all their senses when in his company. What I liked, and very much respected, with David was his normality. He oozes a type of class that I believe only comes from humble beginnings. I was able to make small-talk with him without feeling the need to force it. He offered me a unique insight into life as a youth player with Manchester United when he agreed to be interviewed by me for a special one-off documentary I was co-producing for Manchester United TV about their youth mogul Eric Harrison. Eric is widely known as being the man behind the successful "Class of 92" team which included David, the Neville brothers, Nicky Butt, Ryan Giggs, Paul Scholes and one or two more who went on to have successful careers in the game.

At the time, David's fame was at an astonishing level yet his down-to-earth attitude was unexpected and very much welcomed by me – an unsuspecting lad from a small fishing hamlet in the north-east of Scotland. I left his company that day with a new-found respect for his humbleness. I always respected him as a player and wish him nothing but good fortune for the future. Not that he probably gives a shit what I think!

With Billy it was different. Here was a guy who I grew up with but had never actually seen in the flesh. Could it be as simple as his fame is so vast that I couldn't relate to him on any level? Maybe! With the band, I expected my own level of fame to hit new levels when we were asked to perform on *Top of the Pops*. Our first single "Don't Talk About Love" charted in the top 20 and we were on our way. I allowed the day to pass me by, a decision I regret. It's a surreal experience. I grew up watching the show and my musical tastes formed through observing many a brilliant performance. For me, it was just another day to get through, do our best and hopefully leave a lasting impression. Not for one moment did it ever sink in that I was actually performing on *Top of the Pops*!

I believe the foundation for that thinking was set when the security guards at the gates to Elstree Studios refused Tony and I access. They refused to believe that we were members of an act booked to perform on the show. The fact that we drove to the studios in Tony's clapped-out old Ford Fiesta probably didn't help. It took the fans swarming the car and screaming the place down for the guards to realise that we were actually two members of a boy band! The day after the show aired, I fully expected to be recognised more often. This did not materialise, initially, to my disappointment but looking back it was most definitely for the best.

The foundations had been set for our success, or so I believed. I expected everything to naturally fall into place but how wrong could I be. Our second single "Whenever You Need Someone" charted in the top 30 but I was extremely disappointed by the choice of song. In the music industry, you have to keep the momentum going; you cannot rest on your laurels. After "Don't Talk About Love" charted in the top 20 it was important for me that we achieved a higher chart position with our second single. I wasn't expecting to go straight to number one, or even hit the top 10. But, what I was expecting from the people making the decisions was for the band to make an impact slowly but surely. What I hoped for was a song good enough to enter the charts higher than our debut single. For us to do this the second single had to be even better than the first.

The record company and management took the decision in haste, heavily influenced by "the producer". I found out not long after the decision was made that he wanted this song to be our second single due to the fact it was his mother's favourite track on the album! I was already starting to despair. Now I know this may sound slightly pretentious on my part, thinking I know it all over experienced record company executives, but being in a boy band differs hugely to being in a band like U2 or the Arctic Monkeys. For a start, boy bands thrive on marketing and for this I could not fault our PR department at A&M Records as we just about dominated all radio stations and TV shows going on three years.

For me, Bad Boys Inc was a visual band; we did not play instruments or write hit records. Matthew and David both wrote songs and produced on the odd occasion but they certainly weren't Lennon and McCartney. Matthew experimented with our tracks and helped remix them for our concerts. When better-known artists remixed our tracks, the end results, on more than one occasion, outdid the original. I have often wondered where Bad Boys would have ended up if we had used the remixed versions instead of the ones that were eventually released as singles. We'll never know! We worked extremely hard on our shows, as it was important for all of us that we sent people home impressed enough to come back for more. If we were not gigging or doing promotional work it was not uncommon to see us frequent the Pineapple Dance studios in Covent Garden, or Dance Attic in either Fulham or Oxford Street. We would spend hours rehearsing our shows to the point of exhaustion.

This is what I believe gave us our relative success, the determination to prove people wrong in the industry and make the best of what we could with the Bad Boys Inc sound behind us. Our image played a massive part; we grew quickly as a band and became a strong unit. One of my proudest moments was when we were voted the "Best Dressed Band" by readers of *BIG* magazine at the beginning of 1995. After we charted with our second single the demand for the band grew. We appeared on more TV shows as the requests for interviews doubled and all of a sudden we were deemed as the country's third most popular boy band, behind Take That and East 17. This meant our workload doubled. Below is an actual tour itinerary leading up to the release of our third single, "Walking On Air".

November 1993:

2nd: Confettis nightclub Leeds.
6th: Leeds shopping centre PA, Ritzy nightclub. Limited
      Editions nightclub, Mansfield.
7th: Tuxedo Royals nightclub, Newcastle upon Tyne
8th: Gravesend Secondary School, Gillingham, Excalibur
      nightclub, Dartford, Zen nightclub
9th: Sawbridge Secondary School, Worcester, Tramps nightclub
10th: Preston, Tokyo Joe's nightclub
12th: Sleaford, Legends nightclub, Lincoln, Ritzy nightclub,
      Sheffield, Roxy nightclub

13th: Redhill, Top Shop PA

14th: Newcastle under Lyme, Hippodrome nightclub,
 Stafford, Colisseum nightclub

15th: Burnley, Angel's nightclub

17th: Southsea, 5th Avenue nightclub

18th: Bridgend Secondary School, Bristol, Parkside nightclub

19th: Swinton Secondary School, Wakefield, Rooftop
 Gardens nightclub

20th: Eastleigh, Martine's nightclub

21st: Blackpool, TV Hits concert

23rd: Bedford Secondary School, Dunstable Ritzy nightclub

24th: Dundee, Virgin megastore PA

25th: Trent FM, Christmas lights PA

26th: Folkstone, Lea's Cliff nightclub

27th: Olympia, Gay Styles exhibition, Ashford, Stour
 Centre PA, Streatham, Bang nightclub

28th: Birmingham Dome, TV Hits concert

29th: Scunthorpe, JJ's nightclub, Mansfield, The Yard nightclub

30th: Romford, Hollywood's nightclub, Brixton, The Fridge
 nightclub

"Walking On Air "was our third single and even though it charted in the top 30, it had become our biggest-selling track to date. The Christmas chart is always extremely difficult with the array of tunes being released by one man and his dog. "Walking On Air" was our first ballad: it was OK. Again, I wasn't a big fan but the song gave us more exposure and it was deemed a success as we stayed in the charts for well over six weeks.

By the beginning of 1994, it was becoming apparent that for BBI to be taken seriously we needed a top 10 hit. Our next single was crucial and listening to the options on offer I had little confidence. A&M Records decided, wisely, that we should postpone until the spring to release the next record. This would give "the producer" time in the studio and for the band to build a fanbase around Europe. Our work schedule remained intense with a gruelling tour schedule coupled with a ferocious PR campaign. The press interest was never far away and I found myself, on more than one occasion, filling the column inches, both good and bad!

Apparently, during my time with the band, I had let my new-found celebrity go to my head and had ordered enough Perrier water to bathe in; this I can assure you is not true. Then, I was supposedly banned from flying with British Airways due to a spat at Heathrow Airport! Again, this was not true although I was stopped from flying on a staff ticket, as I was not suitably dressed. That's fair enough but does it really justify a story in *The Sun*? There was also a story doing the rounds that I had almost died after collapsing on stage and suffered a breakdown due to our work schedule. The last time I looked I am pretty sure I didn't die! We made the front page of *The Daily Star* once for causing mayhem at a concert in Birmingham where, unfortunately, some fans were injured in a crush. The story was somewhat elaborated but there was an element of truth to it. I also read with interest in one tabloid that I was a millionaire; I can assure you this has never been the case. Contrary to belief I have never lived in a ten-bedroom mansion, and don't drive a Ferrari or fly in a private jet.

Our fourth single – "More To This World" – was due for release in the middle of May. Leading up to the day of release, we embarked on a nightclub tour that almost sent us to an early grave. We had four months to make sure this record was a top 10 hit. As we travelled up and down the country in our battered VW van, the record company, management and PR worked around the clock to secure as much press coverage as possible. We appeared on numerous TV shows, and just about covered all radio stations the length and breadth of the country. It was a massive undertaking from all involved and the effort put in was astonishing. I can still remember the feeling of exhaustion; gig after gig, interview after interview, one hotel room to another, endless miles of motorway and service stations. Our stage show by this time was running close to half-an-hour and it was still uncommon for us to do less than one gig per night.

Thankfully, we were now in a position to perform in the larger clubs or very small theatres, as the popularity of the band grew. No more dancefloors, smoke-filled rooms or dead-end clubs, we were going up in the world! Thank Christ, "More To This World" charted at number ten in the charts. All the hard work had paid off. I can't begin to tell you the joy and relief that we all felt. At last, I felt we were getting somewhere and stamping our own small mark on the industry. Another performance on *Top of the Pops* beckoned; if we could nail a decent showing maybe, just maybe, the record would sell even more. Rehearsals kicked in and the hard work improving the choreography began in earnest. The next performance could prove to be the most important. We all worked like dogs going through the routine time and time again, step-by-step, move-by-move until perfection was almost achieved.

Thankfully, in the days leading up to *Top of the Pops* our management company cleared our diary so maximum rest was achieved. We, as a band, knew we would have to put on the performance of our lives to make sure "More To This World" continued to rise up the charts. On the morning of the show I was up early, took a walk through the local park, and went through our dance routine in my head time and time again. I was driven to Elstree Studios and hundreds of fans greeted us outside the gates. It added to the excitement! Once in the relative comfort of our dressing room we discovered we would be performing with Wet Wet Wet whose worldwide hit "Love Is All Around" had still to embark on its record-breaking journey. How bloody brilliant, I thought. Cliff Richard popped in to say hello and offer invaluable advice. Cliff Richard, for Christ sake!!! After a quick rehearsal, dress rehearsal and a bite to eat, we were ready for the live performance!

The performance went swimmingly, as far as I was concerned, without a glitch to report. All moves were executed to perfection. It turned out to be a good day all round. Next – the waiting game! In 1994, *Top of the Pops* aired on a Thursday night so we had to wait until the Sunday morning before discovering our fate; had the record moved further into the top 10, or had sales stopped completely? It was a tense few days. When Sunday morning arrived the lads and I all decided to meet at our management office in Hammersmith. We all paced around waiting for the phone call that could make or – in my opinion – break us. When our manager Oliver disappeared into his office to take the dreaded call we all sat round the boardroom table chewing our nails. Oliver reappeared and through a big grin conveyed the very same message he had just taken – we had climbed to number eight in the charts! We all screamed with delight and grabbed each other, congratulating all on a fantastic effort. I called my Mum and Dad immediately and told them the exciting news! I couldn't quite believe it – Bad Boys Inc were at number eight in the charts! What a moment that was, even as I write I am smiling to myself remembering that glorious day. Take That must have been quaking in their boots!

For me, there was no real rivalry as Take That were miles ahead of us in every sense and we simply could not compete with them while our "producer" was at the helm. I respected them for the job they did and if we had had half their success I reckon I would go to my grave a very happy man. I have met the lads a few times and I instantly liked Mark Owen and Robbie Williams but it would be unfair for me to comment on the other lads as I have not been in their company long enough to form an opinion. I had huge respect for their manager, Nigel Martin-Smith. He had taken five lads and nurtured them into the biggest pop sensation since the Bay City Rollers; I openly admit I was envious.

I was asked recently what I felt about Take That reforming and going on to break all records with their 2011 stadium tour? To be honest, I have no feelings. Robbie rejoining is marketing at its very best. Robbie with failing album sales needed Take That as much as Take That needed Robbie. I wish them every success but I don't look on in envy, why would I? They all look great and have obviously kept relatively fit over the years but that doesn't make me want to reform BBI. The TT lads had already made their money and rightly so, why not make a few quid more I say.

You may or may not be surprised to learn that we, as a band, have had one or two offers over the years to reform – the latest being talk of Bad Boys Inc reforming for ITV's popular television show *The Big Reunion*. When word reached me of this particular reality TV show I could not help but be slightly intrigued. The concept of the programme is simple, yet compelling: five different bands from the 1990s reform for a fly-on-the-wall TV show and then head off on a nationwide tour. To be brutally honest, I would rather stick a splintered skewer through my testicles than appear on a television show like that. I have no problems if Matthew, David and Tony wish to reform the band to appear but this is not for me. I mean this with the greatest respect to the producers of the programme and all involved but I have worked too hard for too long to regain any sort of credibility and I believe rightly or wrongly that appearing on the show would do me more damage than good.

To some this may sound slightly arrogant on my part but unless you have experienced what I have you are in no position to judge. Anyway, I won't be able to bust out those dance moves due to one's dodgy knee and God knows what my singing voice sounds like these days considering I have not sung for going on 20 years – therefore you should probably thank me for not wanting to appear on the show!

To be very frank I struggle to understand why some who appeared on that show allowed their souls to be bared for the sake of television. I do have common ground with these people so to a degree I understand what they went through but for goodness sake have some dignity! Nearly all turned to alcohol or drugs (that old chestnut) and some fell into depression. That, I am sorry for, but there is life after boy band/girl bands so strength of character obviously determines the desire to get on with life, or live in the past. I could not help but feel the majority of people on the show continue to cling on to some sort of hope that their 15 minutes of fame will return in some form. Personally speaking, the only band to come out with their credibility intact was the three lads from 911. Lee Brennan, in particular, came across very well and I wish nothing but continued success for these lads. They have seized an opportunity and for that I wish them well. On the other hand I did once find myself getting angry at an interview I read with a former member of a very well known and successful boy band who complained of having to file for bankruptcy after allegedly earning a very decent crust during the band's heyday. After struggling to find his way in the world of showbusiness after the boys went their separate ways he found himself falling into debt. Here's my advice – go and get a fucking job like the rest of us!

The only positive aspect of that whole *Big Reunion* talk was the fact that I rekindled my friendship with my former boy band colleague Tony Dowding after a 20-year period of not talking to each other. I also met up with Matthew on a trip home to London where I was delighted to discover we had no problems starting where we left off all those years ago. David and I continue to talk regularly and I am thrilled he is slowly becoming a renowned actor, director and film producer. One day I would very much like for us all to meet up and enjoy each other's company again but certainly not in the full glare of the general public on a deviously edited television show. Just for the record, I have also been asked to appear on *Never Mind the Buzzcocks* and when MTV poorly attempted to make a reality show by forming a new boy band filled with members of boy bands from days gone by I politely, yet firmly, declined their offers. I shall leave all of that to those who, in my opinion, are nothing but desperate.

Back to the story. Bad Boys Inc enjoyed relative success overseas as our records made the pop charts all over Europe. It wasn't long before we were flying off left, right and centre to promote the band in Germany, Sweden, Denmark, France, Holland, Belgium, Spain and Japan. The latter was an experience I will never forget, as it was mayhem from the minute we arrived until the minute we left! Fans in Japan differ in so many ways from fans in Europe. I met many a fan along the way, collectively and individually, and for the most part I was able to hold down a conversation with most. In Japan, if I was faced with an individual fan I found them incredibly polite, humble and very shy but place that very same fan in a pack and my God the change in personality was frightening. They became hysterical and I don't mean funny! Can this behaviour be put down to some sort of pack mentality, almost animal-like? Did the fans encourage each other to be as crazy as possible, did they vie amongst themselves to be the most outrageous, or was there genuine competition to be "number one fan"? I guess only the fans have the answers to those questions.

My fondest trip with the band was to Hawaii in August 1994. We had recently enjoyed our first top 10 hit with "More To This World" and the record company decided to treat us to first class on Virgin Atlantic through Los Angeles as a thank you for all the hard work we had put in over the past 12 months. Upon our arrival in Honolulu, I marvelled at the paradise I now found myself in. Unable to sleep due to the jet lag I decided, along with the band's photographer Julian Barton, to take a walk down to the beach. The sun was just coming up over the horizon and as Julian and I sat on the beach I suddenly found myself lost in my own thoughts. How had a normal working-class boy from Newburgh in the north-east of Scotland reached the giddy heights of relative fame as a member of a boy band? Over the three-and-a-half years in the public eye, I thought about this many times and felt quite blessed I was doing such a job but the doubts, by that time, had already set in. I was not enjoying the attention, I felt uncomfortable going out, I hated it when people asked me for an autograph. I can't really explain this but I felt very embarrassed in front of people who clearly had no idea who I was, signing a piece of paper, or having my picture taken. On our documentary video this is captured during a trip to Sweden where, quite clearly, I can be seen cowering from the attention.

We spent a total of 12 days in Hawaii shooting two music

videos; one for an upcoming single "Love Here I Come" and a very sultry, sexy number for the record that was due to be our first single from our second album, *Change Your Mind*. I loved the place, the people, the luxurious resort and everything that went with such a trip. It was also a welcome break from the madness back home, and the gruelling tour schedule that was becoming the norm. This was probably the only time "luxury" made itself known to the band.

After our first top 10 hit, the demand for the band grew, be it from press requesting interviews, to appearing on the most popular television shows such as Cilla Black's *Surprise Surprise*, the *Des O'Connor Show*, the *Big Breakfast*, *Noel's House Party* and the *ITV Movie Awards*, to name but a few. It was unusual not to be recognised everywhere we went. Even during a rare day off, if I took a trip into London or went football training, people would come over and say hello. It was all very flattering but, as I said before, I was uncomfortable with it all. I was happy to engage fans in conversation about the band but I did ask them to respect my privacy.

As I was also in a relationship at the time, I wanted my girlfriend to remain anonymous. I lived in St Albans for a year before the fans discovered where I lived. A few had the courage to turn up outside the house and park themselves on my lawn. This, I have to say, infuriated me and I was quite stern in my request for them to leave! As I said, I was happy to chat when I was working but when I am in the privacy of my own surroundings, I wanted to be left alone. I never attended celebrity parties unless we, as a band, had to be there; I never went to a movie premiere unless, again, we as a band had to be there. To me it was all nonsense, contrived nonsense at that!

Eventually, I was forced to move as more and more fans

turned up outside my house. Thankfully, my girlfriend was away working so she never had to face them, but I was extremely uncomfortable. My haven had become my prison so I took the decision to move further into Hertfordshire. After a few weeks searching I eventually found a lovely maisonette in the quaint village of Brookmans Park. Not once was I pestered in the seven years I lived there. Our fourth single "Take Me Away" was an up-tempo number but again, like before, I reserved judgement. It was OK but I honestly believed a remix was needed to modernise the sound. Still, I liked the dance routine and the band's styling for the record and had high hopes for it. In the week of the launch you have an indication of how well the record is selling by the midweek chart – an unofficial chart not released to the public but which insiders take very seriously. We had once again embarked on a mini-tour to promote the record, hit the press between the eyes and kept the momentum going right up until the release date. Upon hearing the news from our management, it would not be an understatement to say we all screamed with joy in a café-bar in the middle of Covent Garden!

The midweek chart position had us in the top five! We were all delighted and knew if sales continued as they did, we should have another top 10 hit. The problem with this is the majority of BBI fans buy the record in the first few days – hence the high sales figures and strong charting position. To continue the momentum we needed the sales to continue throughout the week. This, I feared, would not happen and we would be caught up by other acts. Our sales in the final few days were poor which meant our chart position dropped and we eventually charted officially at number 15. It was still another top 20 hit but I had to confess to being extremely disappointed. We had lost the initiative! Saying that, another performance on *Top of the Pops* beckoned with what I believe was our best performance to date. If you don't believe me, check it out on YouTube!

Our album did not sell well and yet, as perverse as this may sound, I was delighted! This gave us the perfect ammunition to go to "the producer" and tell him we needed to move on as an act and experiment with other producers. The album charted at number ten after we received the incredible news that the midweek chart had us at number one. I strongly believe A&M records were also disappointed and now faced the reality of losing a fair few quid on the first album due to poor sales. This is not uncommon in the music industry as it can take years for a band to recoup the money invested by the label.

At this time A&M were in close and secret negotiations with our management to sign us directly, and not be involved with a third party, as in "the producer". As a band, we could not contain our excitement but we were sworn to secrecy. I loved all this James Bond malarkey! We carried on as normal. By the time our album had been released the popularity of the band had reached new heights. We were very much in demand, not just from the press in the UK, but also abroad, and it wasn't long before we embarked on a major European tour. It was an incredible time meeting new people and visiting new places but the workload was intense.

I also could not help but notice the fans in mainland Europe were very intense to the point of demanding! We always did our best to give back time to our fans and engage with them but at times it became too much to bear. At signing sessions they insisted on phone numbers, addresses, items of clothing, personal belongings etc to the point where it was bordering on obsession. The more this happened the more I started to shy away from the fans. At times, and I stress it was only on the odd occasion, fans would get angry with us if we didn't do as they requested as in signing picture after picture, or having photographs taken from every angle. I remember walking away from one fan and she became hysterical. Screaming at me, calling me names, but as soon as I approached her she calmed down and went on her way – I was left baffled! I also felt guilty. This was a new emotion creeping up on me and I wasn't particularly ready for it.

I fully appreciate and understand that the fans put us where we are; they dictate our level of success. Ultimately, they buy the records, thus providing potential fame and fortune. I get it, but does that mean I should feel guilty for walking away from an overly emotional fan? Between September 1994 and February 1995, Bad Boys Inc released one further song "Love Here I Come". We had shot the video in Hawaii but that was the only good thing about that song. The lads and I were very vocal in our reservations about this record being released in its finished format. Like the others, I felt it was dated and needed bringing into the 20th century.

Matthew and David had done their best to remix the track for our live shows and thank God they did, as at least it sounded more authentic. We needed to have one final hit before the second album, leave the public eye for a while, and return with a bang in the New Year. Did it materialise like this? Did it hell! "Love Here I Come" charted at number 26 and disappeared without trace. It was a huge blow and a sign of things to come. I knew we were on a slippery slope when the producers of the *Smash Hits* Roadshow did not invite us on tour.

If it hadn't been for the intervention of the record company, our PR manager Carolyn Norman and 1st Avenue Management, our relationship with the magazine would have sunk to its lowest ebb. I thank them for their powers of persuasion as the show's producers did a U-turn and invited us along after all! We opened the show and without trying to blow smoke up our own backsides, set the tone for the other acts to follow, one of which was a new boy band by the name of Boyzone! I first became aware of the boys from Ireland when our manager called us into his office one day and offered us "a laugh". We all sat down and watched a VHS recording of what can only be described as the funniest performance I have ever seen of any pop act. The video was recorded on a rooftop somewhere in Ireland with seven lads of varying height, weight and appearance. All were dancing and singing to an old Motown classic. The lads were in stitches and even our manager was crying with laughter. I can clearly recall saying, during a fit of giggles, that if those boys make it and become more successful than us, then we might as well pack it all in and go home, never to return to the music scene again. How those words would come back to haunt me!

During the 1994 *Smash Hits* Tour, I sat with Ronan Keating at the back of the tour bus and reassured him his band would go on to have great success with their first single, and probably after that too. He gave me a sneaky listen to their album and I was overcome with jealousy, as their ballads were simply outstanding – beautifully written and composed. I knew there and then that we as a band were finished! Boyzone had just smashed all records with their debut single "Love Me For A Reason" and were well on their way to becoming one of the world's most popular acts. By this time, I was seriously fed up with it all and wanted out. I found the interviews and photoshoots tedious. It was all so mundane. I appreciate this may come across as slightly selfish and ungrateful but I felt we were constantly battling the system. I was sick of not having any money and struggling to pay my bills. It was a ridiculous situation to be in considering the Bad Boys Inc Company was turning over a small fortune. We as directors were entitled to some sort of dividend but it was never forthcoming. The financial implications of what was happening to us were huge and we as young lads should never have been put in that position. At the beginning of 1995 I believed a light at the end of a long tunnel was in sight and our fortunes were about to change. "The producer", to his credit, had penned a beautifully crafted ballad called "Change Your Mind". This track was set to be our first single from the second album. At this time I understood from those close to us that A&M Records were negotiating with our management to involve other producers for the second album. Our first album in terms of sales performed poorly. This in my opinion was always going to be the end result due to poor production values. For the second album the MD of A&M Records argued our case for the need of a much improved sound. Our "producer" was not for relenting and wanted full control even when he was offered an executive producer's title. He was not for budging, and this, coupled with mismanagement and arrogance from those that should have known better, resulted in the record company dropping us as an act as they refused to record another album with our "producer". I was devastated.

By the end of March/beginning of April 1995, I decided to leave the band for good. To leave it all behind was without doubt in my mind the best option. I spoke to a few of the guys at A&M records whom I had befriended and their guidance and advice was invaluable. I would like to state for the record that A&M records acted honourably throughout and even when they dropped us as an act they waived our debt, even if we signed another deal. I honestly believe the staff appreciated the hard work done by the four of us and that we did everything we could to make the band a success. I don't think David, Matthew, Tony or I could have done any more to build relations with all we came into contact with. Our relationship with the press was strong and amicable. From day one we knew our path would be fraught with difficulty. We did our best when so much was against us. I always felt throughout there was a feeling of inevitability – almost resignation that we were doomed to failure. Who knows what would have happened if the tracks produced on the quiet without "the producer's" knowledge had actually been released – you never know, we may have actually been more successful than we were. Alas, we will never know. It was obviously never meant to be. C'est la vie.

I was left with nothing, not a single penny. The Bad Boys Inc Ltd Company was turning over tens of thousands of pounds every month. You may be astonished to learn that my NET earnings during my time with the band equalled £16,000 over a three-year period. I earned £800 per month, which we paid ourselves via the company. So where did all the money go? I have my own thoughts on this but I shall keep my opinion to myself and hold my counsel. Money is not the be all and end all. Bad Boys Inc released six singles over a three-year period. We charted with all of them, the most popular at number eight, and our worst at number 26. We were the first-ever band to appear on the *National Lottery* show and we officially opened the Big One rollercoaster at Blackpool Pleasure Beach. We smashed television viewing figures in Japan when we performed "More To This World" and won two Best Newcomer Awards in Finland and Denmark. We appeared on *Top of the Pops* four times. I am grateful for the opportunity and look back at it all with a great deal of fondness. The lads and I shared many laughs and good times together and that is what I will take from the crazy time in my life which was Bad Boys Inc – may it rest in peace!

The turning point

The 1995 Coca Cola League Cup Final will forever remain ingrained in my memory, not for the fact Aberdeen won a trophy for the first time in five years but for the horrific abuse I was subjected to by a few mindless Dundee fans during the game. Only a few months before Bad Boys Inc officially split up and I was going through a horrendous time with the financial implications of doing such an act. I was already neck-deep in post-pop-star abyss and had no idea how to escape. Maybe Hampden with my family for another cup final would help me forget, even if it was for just a few hours?

Aberdeen's route to the final was fairly straightforward with comfortable wins in the first two rounds against St Mirren and Falkirk. The quarter-final against Motherwell at Fir Park went to extra time before John Inglis grabbed a late winner. That set up a midweek semi-final tie with Scottish champions Rangers at Hampden Park. Rangers, at the time, were dominating Scottish football with an excellent team containing stars like Paul Gascoigne, Ally McCoist and Brian Laudrup. I toyed with the idea of travelling to Glasgow for the game but in the end decided to stay down south and watch it in the pub over the road. I was still waiting for my satellite dish to be installed so I headed over to the local pub to have a shandy and watch the game from a barstool.

With the game being played on a Wednesday night, the attendance at Hampden that evening was poor. I sometimes wonder why the authorities governing our game make such decisions; surely it would have made more sense to play the game at the weekend? For a start, the hordes of Dons fans, who would have travelled down on a Saturday or Sunday, could not do so in midweek because of work and family commitments. So, not surprisingly, the majority of fans on display that evening were those from the blue side of Glasgow town... how convenient! But, I do applaud those Dons fans determined to cheer the boys on from Hampden and making the extra effort to be there.

I enjoyed the game from the relative comfort of a bar lounge and marvelled at the display from the Dons. Eoin Jess and Paul Bernhard in particular were outstanding, dominating Gazza throughout. When Billy Dodds opened the scoring for Aberdeen it took all my might not to scream the place down but by the time the second went in I couldn't control myself; I was off the stool in a blink of an eye punching the air shouting "get in". The former Tottenham striker Martin Chivers – who owned the pub – asked me politely to take my seat and keep the noise down as he had paying customers; I sheepishly apologised. Even when Rangers scored late on, I still had every confidence we could see the game out. When the full-time whistle blew, I was elated and decided there and then I was going to the final. With all the stress I was under at the time, the emotional release was overwhelming. While everyone else in the pub that night had watched a meaningless football match, for me it meant a great deal. Mr Chivers even bought me a shandy to toast our success!

I spoke to my Dad that very same evening and told him we should all go, as we had not attended a final as a family for a while. I had to wait less than a month for the Coca Cola Cup Final. I flew direct to Glasgow from London. My gran was delighted to see me after a good couple of years being away on tour; the feeling was mutual. I spent a wonderful evening in Bishopbriggs catching up with everyone and telling my tale. I had not felt this relaxed for months. The day of the match itself was a dreary November afternoon. I was really looking forward to going to Hampden as the grand old stadium had recently been refurbished and I was yet to attend a game in the newly built arena. Upon our arrival a few Dons fans came over and said hello, a few quite obviously had a laugh at my expense, all in good humour which I thoroughly enjoyed but all in all the banter was in full flow. When we entered the stadium I was fairly impressed, it was so different to the old Hampden but modern times dictate modern architecture.

As we took our seats I sheepishly signed a few autographs and had my photograph taken with a few Bad Boys fans. By this time, the banter was at an all-time high and I was having a great time being back amongst the Red Army. Even though there was still this ridiculous element of celebrity around me, I had not felt so normal in such a long time. As we took our seats I noticed we were sitting almost on top of the Dundee fans. Only a few rows separated them from us. I wasn't particularly fussed but I was mindful of their presence as the excitement levels rose ahead of kick-off. The atmosphere was electric and with the PA system banging out the tunes it all added to the fun.

The Dons' opponents were First Division side Dundee. I was a tad nervous going into the game as Aberdeen were red-hot favourites. Anything can happen in cup finals but my nerves soon settled as the Dons dominated the game from the off and never looked in any danger of losing. Billy Dodds opened the scoring, which was met by the usual Begg family celebration. I was engrossed in the game but was aware of a group of lads to my right in the Dundee section who were making noises about a lad from a boy band! I glanced over and was met with a few comments and wanker signs from one or two of them; "Hey you, ye fucking poof," "Haw Ally, you're a fucking cunt." I glanced over, offered a wry smile and carried on watching the game.

As half-time approached more and more Dundee fans had recognised me and were hell-bent on giving me what for. To be honest, I wasn't that bothered until we reached half-time. During the break a couple of girls came over and asked for a picture and an autograph. This act seemed to anger the small pocket of Dundee fans and the abuse became more personal. "Begg, you shag men" was one such expletive that sticks out. Another one which almost made me laugh was; "You're no famous, you're a fucking con artist." I would like to make it clear at this point it was only a handful of fans dishing out the abuse as I'm sure the majority couldn't give a shit about some lad from a boy band; I would like to think they were there to enjoy their team play in a cup final just as much as we were.

Over the past few years I had been on the end of many a disgruntled rant, be it from a jealous boyfriend in a nightclub whose girlfriend was watching us on stage or someone who decided to place me on a pedestal and take an instant dislike to me. A thick skin was required but I can safely say I was never particularly bothered by such drivel. For three years I had to endure, on more than one occasion, when popping out for a pint of milk, or going into London to shop or whatever the case may be people yelling "poof", or "wanker". Now and then I became affectionately known as "faggot" but my particular favourite had to be "fucking boy band twat". I remember being in Miami to shoot the video for "More To This World" and as we took a gentle stroll down the strip I overheard some poor guy saying; "I've come all the way to fucking Miami and fucking Bad Boys Inc are here." I admit the comment made me stop in my tracks and have a right good laugh. I hope we didn't spoil the poor lad's holiday! At times it really was quite amusing but the humour stopped that day at Hampden.

My Mum, Dad and brother, Peter, were all in earshot of what was being said and the language, and the use of it, was appalling. I don't mind bad language now and then, I openly swear myself, but what was being directed that day towards my family went too far. These mindless idiots stepped over the line. My Mum was visibly shaken and on the verge of tears; no mother should have to hear that sort of verbal abuse directed at their son. My Dad on the other hand was quietly boiling inside. My Dad was the most laid-back person I have ever known, normally confronting problems in life with humour and character but his personality changed that day to something I did not recognise.

He stood in silence watching and listening to what was being directed at me and was on the verge of exploding and, this I confess, worried me. I told them all to calm down, not to worry about it and go and get a cup of tea. As we all left some of the Aberdeen fans that were beside us enquired if all was OK. A couple of guys shouted towards the stewards to do something about the Dundee fans. These comments I'm ashamed to say fell on deaf ears. I wish I could meet these fans today and tell them how grateful I am for their actions that afternoon.

As we returned for the second half, some of the fans seated beside us very kindly gave up their seats so we could be further away from the line dividing the two sets of fans. Unfortunately, this did not have the desired affect and the abuse continued. "You're a fucking prick" shouted one lad who looked too young to be using such language! By this stage my brother was getting very agitated and started returning some of the abuse but I pleaded with him to let it go. I know he was only protecting me but I didn't want them to see it was affecting us. As the game continued, Stephen Glass found himself in some space down the left flank and delivered a beautiful ball into the box which Duncan Shearer met with his head and the ball flew into the back of the net, 2–0! I needed no invitation; I barged past my family and the other fans and met the Dundee fans face-to-face and just let rip.

I went berserk, shouting, swearing, screaming at the top of my voice, "come on then, come on ye bunch of fuckers" while punching the air with delight at our second goal. My brother, my Dad and a couple of strangers took hold of me and dragged me back before a riot ensued. I was still screaming and kicking out but my Dad took a hold of me and held me tight whispering in my ear to "calm down", and to "take it easy". His grip was firm and I could feel my brother's hand on the back of my head. I started to cry. I started to sob uncontrollably. In those few seconds in the immediate aftermath of Aberdeen scoring their second and decisive goal, I released all my anger, frustration and emotion that had been building up over the past year or so and directed it all at those few Dundee fans. Thankfully, the stewards stepped in and the unnecessary abuse stopped.

Looking back, I'm ashamed of my actions as I let myself down. A few around us asked if we were OK, as most folk seemed genuinely concerned. I managed to calm myself down, take a deep breath, and continue watching the game but it went by in a blur. I was so shocked and horrified by the abuse it made me question my motives for joining the band. I convinced myself I joined for the right reasons, to make my immediate family and I financially secure for the rest of our lives. I saw it as the perfect opportunity, as with success comes the trappings. I explained this once to television presenter Terry Christian during an interview not long after I moved to Manchester and he suggested I had prostituted myself.

Don't we all prostitute ourselves to get by though? Why do we do the jobs we do if it isn't to make a living and survive! Terry's use of words that night angered and flustered me. Some may find this difficult to believe, and some who don't actually know me personally may think I am talking out my arse, but I never joined the band to be famous or become a celebrity. All I ever wanted to do in life was become a professional football player, anything else was second best. I understood from day one that becoming famous was par for the course, it came with the job but there was nothing in my job description explaining just how difficult and intrusive it would actually become.

For too long I had watched Mum and Dad work very hard to offer us the type of upbringing that we received. Dad, in particular, went through traumatic experiences with his employers to the point he decided enough was enough and went out on his own. All I wanted to do was take away some of the financial burden, and becoming a pop star offered me the perfect opportunity. Shame it had the opposite effect! That day at Hampden with my family on November 26th 1995 was a turning point in my life. I lost all self-control emotionally and allowed a few morons to get to me; I vowed there and then I would get my life back on track and face the realities of the band splitting up head on. Refusing to bury my head in the sand, I had the option of going one of two ways, either feeling sorry for myself or just cracking on with my life; thankfully I decided to take the latter option. That game against Dundee means so much to me on a personal level. It represented a significant turning point in my life – it was the last time, as a family, we were all together for a final as my beloved Dad passed away suddenly on June 1st 2007.

Getting back on track

In the immediate aftermath of leaving the band I needed to take some time out to decide where to go next. For the previous two years I had played football regularly for the Arsenal Ex-Professional and Celebrity Football XI and fallen in love with playing all over again. I decided to try and forge a career in the game. After consulting a friend of mine at the Scottish Football Association he advised me to take my Scottish Football Association coaching badges; little did I know at the time that guiding me through the courses would be three Aberdeen legends!

The SFA coaching courses differ today from what they were back in 1995. I completed the Development Coaching Certificate over a weekend in the company of former Aberdeen midfielder Neil Simpson. It was a treat for me to be up close and personal with a player who I had always idolised. I did my best to impress him and the other participants who quite obviously were slightly perplexed to be in the company of a boy band star on a football-coaching weekend! However, I quickly bonded with all the guys and thoroughly enjoyed the weekend from start to finish. I passed the course with the help of Neil and could not be more impressed with his technique, not just on a coaching level but on a personal level too. He treated everybody the same and offered much encouragement throughout. Two months later I was back in Aberdeen for a week-long course to try and gain the more difficult Club Coach Badge. In the intervening period between the two courses I visited Neil at Pittodrie and picked his brains about all things coaching. I had ideas of grandeur of maybe getting a job at Pittodrie and one day becoming first-team coach.

The club coach course was held on the playing fields of Aberdeen's Northern College and conducting the course were two former Aberdeen greats, Drew Jarvie and Chic McClelland. I had met Drew previously and liked him immensely; here I was in the company of one of Aberdeen's all-time greatest players and current first-team coach. Time to impress, not just from a coaching point of view but if I played well in the arranged games, maybe he would have a word and sign me! I saw myself running out at Pittodrie in the very next game wearing the number 10 shirt and scoring a sensational 25-yard winner against Rangers!

Back to reality! Chic was an excellent coach and mentor; he played over two hundred games for the Dons in the 1970s and was employed by the club to guide the careers of the next generation of Aberdeen players. I had a fantastic five days learning new coaching techniques and taking my own experience to another level. The lessons learned were invaluable and both Chic and Drew encouraged me to follow a path in the game. Over the next 12 months I continued to travel to Aberdeen from my home in Hertfordshire and attend the various SFA courses and seminars. I kept in touch with Drew for many years but after he left Pittodrie we have lost touch. I sincerely hope he is well and enjoying life; without realising it, he helped me through a very difficult period in my own life and for that I will always be grateful to him. As for Neil Simpson, I have watched his career flourish. Whenever I pop into Pittodrie I always make a beeline for his office; he is a great man and I have no doubt one day he will become a great manager, be it at our club or another!

Just for the record, I did put my qualifications to use over many a summer working for the Arsenal Soccer Schools and, indirectly, when my life took a change for the better in the early part of 1999. As I continued to study the game with the help of the SFA I was also playing on a regular basis. Every Sunday afternoon I would turn out for the Arsenal Celebs and travel all over the country playing in charity games. It was a fantastic distraction from the financial problems I was facing. The side was run by a gentleman called Alan Sefton, who headed up the community programme for Arsenal Football Club. The side was managed by former Arsenal kit manager, the late Bill Graves. The idea behind the team was to raise as much money as possible through the Arsenal Charitable Trust Fund. Clubs from all over the country made a donation to the charity and we would turn up on the day to play a game. Over the years we raised hundreds of thousands of pounds for various charities, something I am very proud of.

I looked forward every weekend to driving to the games with my mates, former Arsenal midfielder David Court, who also lived in Brookmans Park, and magician Marvin Berglas. Marvin's father David, as a matter of interest, was the president of the Magic Circle and first magician to appear on television. I formed great friendships over the years with many of the lads who played in the side, notably John Alford, who played Billy in *London's Burning*. John and I became very close, especially during the period he was convicted of selling drugs to a "fake sheikh". John's personality went everywhere with him; he was extremely popular with all and took his football very seriously. His moment of stupidity ultimately cost him his wealth and his career. Unfortunately for John, he would not recover. I've not seen or spoken to him for many years now, which makes me sad, as the bond was strong. I sincerely hope he is well and getting on with life.

Another mate of mine was Tony Hadley, the lead singer of Spandau Ballet. What a talent he was. Just as well as he was an awful football player! It was not uncommon for Tony to pick up a mic and bust out a tune after a game and capture the hearts of many a middle-aged lady once again! Tony and I found common ground with the music industry and spent many a late night talking about our trials and tribulations. I'm delighted his problems are behind him with Gary Kemp, and Spandau have reformed, as he is a truly lovely man. Marvin Berglas is a man of unparalleled talent, a magician whose tricks left me and others utterly flabbergasted. Marvin is a passionate Arsenal fan and entertains VIPs ahead of games at the Emirates Stadium; some may suggest there's more magic off the pitch than on when Marvin is around! I was thrilled when, after losing touch for many years, we found each other and the friendship has been rekindled.

As much as I enjoyed playing with many a "celeb" over the years there's nothing better than playing with ex-pros! I was fortunate to share the same dressing room as Brian Talbot, Pat Rice, Brian Hornsby, Martin Hayes, Paul Dickov, Peter Marinello, Ian Allison, Perry Groves, David Jenkins, John Radford, Alan Smith, Paul Davies, Graham Rix, Liam Brady and many others. It was a privilege to play with these guys and made me realise just why I never made it as a pro. They always say you never lose it. Some of these guys were in their fifties and still had the touch of someone 30 years younger. At times it was brilliant to watch and I have no doubts my own game improved by simply playing alongside these guys. I played for the Arsenal Ex-Pros and Celebrity XI for seven years and loved every minute I was with the guys; I miss them all terribly!

Following in the footsteps

My career path shifted again at the beginning of 1999. It had been four years since the split of the band and I was just about back on track. I was earning a decent wage and enjoying relative anonymity. At the time I was managing a small hotel gym on the outskirts of London and out of the blue I received a phone call from a dear friend of mine Andy Sheldon, whom I had met during my time with the band when he was a DJ for Power FM in Portsmouth. Andy and I had performed in a pantomime together during the festive period of 1995 and a firm friendship developed immediately.

Andy had the gift of the gab, and was a fabulous entertainer, so it came as no surprise when Granada Shop in Liverpool called for his services. Back in 1999, Granada Shop was a successful shopping channel selling goods from the Littlewoods catalogue. Andy presented and helped sell a host of products over a weekend and, it has to be said, that after one particular show, his powers of persuasion almost convinced me to buy some cooking pots! One morning, out of the blue, Andy called me and asked if I would be interested in joining the channel as they desperately needed a fitness instructor to help sell the health and fitness equipment. Granada wanted to offer me a trial to start with but I knew there and then I was up for the job. I had always fancied the idea of working in television, and had not forgotten that during my time with the band I had guest presented the Disney Channel and the *Big Breakfast*, so working in a studio environment was not exactly new to me! For the next six months I travelled up and down from Liverpool twice weekly to host the fitness segments, as well as continue my shifts at the gym. As the weeks passed I became more and more confident in my presenting ability and wanted more.

In a chance meeting that summer I was introduced to a young man by the name of Richard Aaron. Richard travelled from Granada headquarters in Manchester to Liverpool to gain some experience ahead of a new project for MUTV – Manchester United's very own official TV station. Richard told me he was looking for a vibrant presenter for a youth magazine show starting in the new football season. I threw my name in the hat immediately! After a few days I found myself doing a screen test for a programme called *Reds@Five* in a small studio at the back of the main Granada Studios in Manchester. That day, the production team wanted me to host with two girls who were also being screen-tested but, as no other guy appeared on the horizon, I thought the gig was as good as mine.

During the show I had to interview two celebrities; Andy Ritchie, former Manchester United and Oldham striker, and Nick Cochrane who played Andy MacDonald in Coronation Street and who is a massive United fan. Over the years Nick and I have become very close friends and I was honoured when he asked me to be his daughter's godfather, a responsibility I do not take lightly. The audition went well and the boss offered me the job that very night; to say I was delirious is an understatement! I was overcome with emotion, overjoyed and BACK! The move to Manchester took no time at all. I rented a room from one of Andy friends in a penthouse apartment at the back of Canal Street and prepared myself for a new beginning. The apartment was magnificent, an industrial conversion with huge bay windows and views of the Manchester skyline. Living there made me feel like a million dollars! It was the first time I had felt like that for years.

The following days were taken up with production meetings and script meetings. I couldn't wait to get started, and when word got round the office that Sir Alex Ferguson had agreed to an interview with us, the excitement reached new levels. The production team interviewed two more girls for the co-host position but I put my foot down one day when this over-exuberant blonde introduced herself to me by saying; "Hello, I used to mime in a band as well!" Cheeky bitch! Thankfully, the team found a wee gem in a former British Airways stewardess called Jeanette Lanz Bergin, or as she was more fondly known, Jeannie B. I liked Jeannie from the off. I loved her energy and her zest for life. She was new to TV, and quite obviously nervous about the whole deal, but she would take to it like a duck to water.

One of our first jobs as the new presenters of *Reds@Five* was to interview Sir Alex at the Cliff, United's former training centre. On the way there my nerves started to get the better of me but I did my best to disguise it. Meeting Sir Alex after all these years was thrilling and when he stepped into the room my heart skipped a beat! Here was the man who was my hero, the man who had guided my team to glories that will never be matched again. He looked smaller than I remembered but he oozed class. I couldn't stop staring at him and Jeannie gently elbowed me in the ribs, which helped me gain my composure!

He came over and introduced himself. As if he had to do that! And I offered him a cheesy grin and introduced myself back. He recognised the accent and asked me where I was from to which I replied "Aberdeen". He asked me if I supported the Dons. I quietly whispered back "passionately!" I then plucked up the courage to tell him my gran was asking after him. I explained who my gran was and as soon as I mentioned my late grandpa he looked me right in the eye and asked if I was John Begg's son.

I explained I was his eldest grandson. He smiled, put his arm round me and told me that grandpa was a great man for whom he had huge respect, and that I should be very proud of him. I swear in that moment, I almost started crying!! Thankfully, I held it together and for the next 20 minutes Sir Alex sat and chatted to me about Aberdeen and football in general. It was an incredible moment and set the benchmark for my relationship with him. After we finished the interview and photo session Sir Alex personally signed a Manchester United shirt for me, which I still have to this day. It was a magical afternoon and without realising it, I had impressed the hierarchy at MUTV so much the boss called me with con-gratulations on a fantastic day's work.

As the months flew by the show improved and I did not hold back in declaring my love for the Dons. In fact, I did not need an excuse to mention them at any given opportunity. At the turn of the millennium, the production team came up with an idea for the show that involved me travelling to Aberdeen to do a special feature on the club. I needed no invitation. So the next thing I know I'm in the car and heading up the M6 to the motherland. The production team had arranged for me to train with the team and interview Aberdeen legend Teddy Scott about his recent testimonial match against Manchester United. On the morning of the shoot, I awoke to clear beautiful skies and relished the day ahead. As I fought my way through the early morning traffic my producer reminded me to remain professional and make the right impression. I confess the butterflies in my stomach were having a field day as my nerves started to get the better of me. Once at Pittodrie we were met by the PR team who gave us the run of the place until we were satisfied all was done.

As the players were due in shortly we took the opportunity to film in and around the ground. This didn't take long so we moved on to Teddy Scott and my interview with this one-off. He was magnificent that day, offering us his precious time and giving me a unique insight into his well-deserved testimonial. Looking around Teddy's room after the interview was a treat and I gazed in wonder at the array of shirts from down the years, as well as the mass of Aberdeen memorabilia he collected over the years. It is literally an Aberdeen Football Club Aladdin's cave.

After concluding the interview it was time to get on my freshly polished boots. I didn't want to be fined for having dirty boots after all! I felt the part but my producer was quick to say I certainly didn't look the part! The players by this time were already training over on the Links near the beach so it was time to join in! As I ran over, Aberdeen's first-team coach Tommy Moller Nielsen told me to get involved in a small-sided game. I needed no invitation, said hello to a couple of the lads, received a pass from Eoin Jess, nutmegged Gary Smith and laid the ball off. I couldn't believe what had just happened, as did the other lads as they all fell about laughing at poor Gary's expense. I felt like the character Billy the Boots from *Roy of the Rovers* as I was unaware I had such an array of skills. It was pure luck or fear on my part! I offered a humble apology to Gary, as I honestly didn't mean to embarrass him. He laughed and said if I could sing as well as I could play football I may have made something of myself!

His words certainly had a calming effect, as I did not put a foot wrong. I had a fantastic time and was living the dream, albeit for 60 minutes or so. The lads were fantastic

– very welcoming and I enjoyed their company throughout. Once the training session was over we made our way back to the ground for some "pieces to camera" on the pitch. My producer set me a challenge to try and do some ball juggling ahead of the scripted piece. As the lads were in the middle of their warm-down round the perimeter track, I felt a little pressure to nail it. Thankfully I did... after three takes and many dropped balls!

As the lads ran past us a few wise-guy jokes about the boy band flowed – all harmless fun! After we completed the filming I hung around and smashed a few balls into the Richard Donald Stand goal, without a goalkeeper being in place and again allowed my over-excited mind to drift. That afternoon at Pittodrie I was like a small child, dreaming of what could have been if I had worked a little harder at my game. The Pittodrie staff were exceptional all morning and helped make the filming process very easy. I'm delighted to say the final product made it to air on MUTV and ran for weeks. That day at Pittodrie, like so many others, will not be forgotten in a hurry.

When Aberdeen reached the Scottish Cup Final in 2000, I decided a trip up the M6 and M74 was a must. The Dons made very hard work of the early rounds and then found themselves facing a semi-final with Hibs. The game was due to be screened live on Sky Sports, which meant a date enjoying my own company in the safe haven of my small apartment in Manchester. I did toy with the idea of driving up but due to work commitments with MUTV this was near impossible.

It's been known at times that I have been rather vocal in my support of the side in important games. It wasn't long after kick-off that my neighbour gently knocked on my door and quietly asked for me to keep the noise down. I promised her

I would do my best but offered no guarantees. When Andy Dow smashed home the winner to book Aberdeen's place in the final, I let rip, jumping all over the apartment, punching the air with delight while screaming at the top of my voice. At full time a swift yet effective apology was delivered to my weary neighbour, which she duly accepted – bless her!

On the eve of the game, I drove up to Glasgow from Manchester and stayed the night with my relatives in Bishopbriggs. I felt a tad sad that Mum, Dad and Peter couldn't make it but I wasn't going to let that ruin what I was hoping would be a great day out. The morning of the game felt slightly strange. There was no over-excitement, no dressing up in replica kits and no kick-about with my younger brother. I'm not ashamed to say I missed that side of it. I was delighted to see so many Dons fans making the effort on the day to get behind their team, especially when the odds were stacked against them. Rangers were the opponents that day and firm favourites to lift the famous old trophy.

As I took my place behind the goal I didn't really know what to expect, as I hadn't actually watched this side live in action before. I had watched games on TV but as we all know it's not quite the same. What I was pleased about was the fact that I would be there for Jim Leighton's final game for the club. Jim had been in goal for my first-ever Dons game and like so many other fans that day we were witnessing the end of a glorious era. I felt almost privileged to have watched this fine goalkeeper in action for nearly 20 years. Unfortunately for Jim, he would make headlines for all the wrong reasons. I clearly recall thinking he was in trouble after the unfortunate collision with Rod Wallace but never did I, or many of the fans around me, appreciate the extent of his injury. As Jim was being carried off, the lad standing next to me said, "You have got to be joking." I looked at him and asked what he was going on about and he told me to look over at the touchline and see who was coming on as our replacement goalkeeper.

I think the shock hit all Dons fans at the same time as a sense of bemusement swept across the vast stand behind Jim Leighton's goal. As Robbie Winters ran on to what was a rapturous ovation, I said to the lad next to me; "We're fucked!" He nodded his head in agreement. For those of you who are unaware of the former Aberdeen and Dundee United striker he is all of five-foot nothing – one of the smallest players in the league at that time! Our manager Ebbe Skovdahl, in his own wisdom, decided a substitute goalkeeper would not be required. Unfortunately, this baffling decision by Mr Skovdahl turned the cup final into a shambles and it wasn't long before Rangers took the lead.

Rangers scored three further goals in the space of about five minutes after the re-start, and that was that as far as I was concerned. I was so distraught that I toyed with the idea of leaving and making my way back to Bishopbriggs but that would have been a very selfish act. Looking back, I'm so pleased I took the decision to stay and continue to cheer the lads on. We all knew the game was beyond reach, so instead of wallowing in pity the Red Army decided it was time to party, and my what a party it was. The fans never stopped singing for the duration of the second half and, it has to be said, out-sang the Rangers fans that smugly watched on. Watching the hundreds of fans doing the hokey cokey up and down the stairwells was a sight to behold, great fun and very funny. I enjoyed that more than the game. Any defeat against Rangers is difficult to stomach but a 4–0 defeat in a cup final left a bitter taste in the mouth. To be honest I didn't hang around for long and took the decision to drive back to Manchester that night.

Years later during my time with Setanta, I was fortunate enough to form a strong friendship with former Dons captain Derek Whyte. When Derek left to build a new life for himself in Dubai with his lovely wife Donna, he offered me his cup final shirt from that fateful day, and his Teddy Scott Testimonial shirt from the game against Manchester United. I'm delighted for Derek that he is doing well in Dubai and has forged a very successful broadcasting career for himself. We talk most weeks and he still keeps a close eye on the results. Just for the record, I humbly accepted his shirts and they hang neatly in my spare room. At the time of writing, the Dons have not contested a Scottish FA Cup Final since that defeat by Rangers. We should have been there in 2008 but the appalling nature of the defeat against Queen of the South meant another catastrophe to get over. It was becoming part of the norm for us Aberdeen fans.

My time at MUTV was well spent. It was my television apprenticeship and I used my time there to learn and develop my skills as a broadcaster. At times it was not easy with an audience ready to pounce on any slip-up or mistake. A thick skin is required and I was not quite ready for some of the criticism that came my way. I had been used to bad press during my time with Bad Boys Inc but the character assassination in the first few months at MUTV was difficult to stomach. Thankfully, I was presenting to a relatively small number of viewers as the subscription levels of the channel grew moderately in the first couple of years. By the time I left in 2004, the subscription levels had grown dramatically to well over 150,000. It was a fantastic learning curve for me, adapting to the world of television and sport. I mastered the art of reading autocue, wearing an earpiece and taking instructions from the director and producer.

At first, having somebody talking to you in your ear while at the same time talking to a guest or the audience can be very off-putting but, thankfully, I was already well-equipped thanks to my time at Granada Shop, so I felt very comfortable multi-tasking! One feature of the job where you can either sink or swim is ad-libbing. This is required at any given time in the programme. Fortunately, I am not known to be short of a word or two so I did not particularly struggle in this department. Once again the shopping channel experience helped me dramatically. If I could offer any aspiring television presenter any advice, begin your apprenticeship with a shopping channel. There is no hiding place; you have to think on your feet, deliver and ad-lib when given instruction. It's a fantastic way to learn the industry and the trade.

To become the very best you MUST be able to ad-lib. Far too many presenters these days rely on autocue and pre-prepared scripts. If the autocue was to fail you will be found out. I have, unfortunately, seen this too many times to mention and it's painful to watch. Unfortunately, when watching TV if something goes wrong the general public automatically believes it must be the presenter's fault, it's human nature. The buck stops with the host. Most people – and I mean this with the greatest respect – don't see the machine behind the scenes. Let's not forget the production staff, director, sound engineer, tape operator, runner, vision mixers, graphic operators, camera operators and so on and so on. So here's my point, if I can speak for 20 minutes and convince a viewer to buy a pair of running socks I am sure I can talk about football for a few seconds! Most of the shows on MUTV required nothing but ad-libbing, except for the half-hourly news bulletins which all ran off autocue.

I particularly enjoyed shows such as *United in Press* where two Manchester-based journalists would be invited into the studio to discuss all the latest United topics. Having seasoned pros such as Steve Bates, who chairs the National Football Writers' Association, and James Fletcher, who wrote brilliant football stories for the now defunct *News of the World*, was insightful, as much as it was entertaining. To be able to pick these guys' brains and discover why they report in the manner they do is not just informative for the viewer, but it made me realise that in the studio my questions have to be thought-out and delivered with aplomb. There is no hiding place for a presenter if they do not think on their feet. All must master the art of listening to the guest to be able to instantly react to their views to be able to take the conversation forward, while at the same time take instructions from producer, director and others in the gallery! Thankfully, most of the presenters I have worked with over the years have been able to execute this quite brilliantly but some have not, and this is where they let themselves down.

Interviewing the players was a thrill, as much as it was challenging. My questions had to be thought out carefully. I will elaborate on this later, but one had to be very careful with one's line of questioning. My priority with all the players was comfort. I needed them to trust me. As much as I needed to get the information out of them, pushing players when you represent the official club channel is a very fine art. The party line has to be adhered to. My grandpa's legacy, and that of my uncle, has always followed me in my television career and I refuse, under any circumstances, to change my style. Sir Alex Ferguson once said to me – do not change – I won't! If a player or coach, or any representative of Manchester United, Celtic, Aberdeen, or whoever I worked for, or had close contact with, said "this does not go any further" I gave them my word it would not. If I betrayed their trust this book would not be written in the manner it has. I make no apology for this. I will never sell my soul down the river to make a few quid.

It makes me very proud that players over the years have talked openly to me and felt comfortable in my presence. Building trust in any walk of life is important but in that particular stage of my career it was a given. I always tried to make the player as comfortable as possible prior to the cameras rolling. Talking to the players about everyday life, family or even the weather was all part of the bigger plan to offer a relaxed atmosphere which duly led to a better and more insightful interview. Some players were better in front of camera than others, so those that were camera shy needed encouragement and guidance. Players such as Gary Neville, Phil Neville, Ryan Giggs, Ole Gunnar Solskjaer and Wes Brown were naturals. Players like goalkeeper Roy Carroll, Paul Scholes, or the foreign lads, needed encouragement. Dwight Yorke was great fun and always ready for a laugh. Andy Cole was mysterious. Roy Keane I will save for later in the book! Which brings me nicely to Sir Alex!

As I mentioned at the top of the chapter, when I met Sir Alex at Carrington in my early days with MUTV it was nothing short of thrilling. During my time with the company I had the pleasure of interviewing him three times. On each occasion he greeted me with a big grin and a firm handshake. He once even put his arm round me! I nearly fainted! I knew our time together would be short so I tried to make the most of it. Interviewing Sir Alex is like nothing I have ever experienced before. His style, knowledge and demeanour meant stepping up my game. I don't know why this happened, and I can't really explain it on paper, but in my eyes I was in the company of greatness which meant I did not want to disappoint him, or more importantly annoy him or piss him off. He is nothing short of captivating. Questions had to be carefully delivered and thought of to the point where insulting his football brain was the ultimate sin. In the days leading up to the interview I would spend time carefully scripting my questions and thinking how I could actually captivate him! Some may laugh at this, and question why this was not done with all I came in contact with, but Sir Alex is in a different league – he is the boss in more ways than one!

On each occasion he was late, which added to my already shattered nerves. During my time with MUTV, he was always on the go. He never appeared to have a minute to himself. The last time I interviewed him, when I joined Celtic, he greeted me like an old friend, slumped in his seat and said; "Let's have a cup of tea first." At first it took me a couple of seconds to comprehend that he wanted to just sit and collect his own thoughts while sat in my company. I took that as a huge compliment! He spoke of my grandpa and asked how I was getting on at Celtic. He appeared genuinely interested. I didn't want it to end! When my Dad died so very suddenly in 2007, imagine my surprise when a letter arrived for me at the Setanta offices from Sir Alex. He had learned of my father's death and penned a beautifully written letter offering his utmost condolences. His words will remain private but I will forever hold that letter close to my heart as it meant so much. His kindness was in some small part a comfort to me, my Mum and my brother Peter.

When I came up with the idea for this book many, many years ago I only wanted one person to write the foreword, but I always feared it would never happen. I knew it would take a huge effort on my part to gain the trust of Sir Alex.

I am fortunate my grandpa opened a door which allowed me to forge a relationship with him. He trusted me from the off knowing my morals and standards matched those of my grandpa. Those very same morals are still very much in evidence today in my current role. I am not arrogant enough to believe Sir Alex is a friend of mine, he is not. I am insignificant to him but I am grateful that I can call upon him. I have, over the years, written to him twice to ask for his advice which he duly offered. When it came to the foreword I thought long and hard how to approach him. I decided the best course of action was simply to chance my luck so one afternoon during a quiet moment when Lennox enjoyed his afternoon nap I wrote to him via the senior press officer at Manchester United Football Club and waited to see what would develop. I didn't have to wait long!

Five days later, while writing this very book, an email popped into my inbox. I confess I hesitated to open it in fear of what I was expecting. The reply said; "Hi Ally, Sir Alex has agreed to do this for you." I couldn't believe it – I had to read it twice for my brain to compute the enormity of what those 11 little words actually said! He had agreed to write the foreword. I swear I almost screamed with joy. I ran into the kitchen where Miriam was busy preparing dinner. I almost couldn't get the words out for excitement. I was on the verge of hyperventilating – as dramatic as that sounds! Miriam stopped what she was doing, hugged me and whispered "well done" in my ear. I could tell she was thrilled for me without fully understanding what this gesture meant to me. As much as I am grateful to all the former players who have contributed to this book, to have Sir Alex write the foreword for me is without doubt one of the greatest thrills of my life. What a legend!

I have nothing but fond memories of my time with MUTV.

I forged friendships which remain to this day, notably Campbell Gray, who was my first-ever news producer and the man I credit with turning me into the presenter I eventually became. The channel is a superb servant to the Manchester United fans and has improved dramatically over the years, with some superbly produced documentaries and features. I applaud their marvellous efforts. When it came to leaving, the decision was almost made for me!

Welcome to the family

In the summer of 2004, my broadcasting career took a turn for the better when all seemed lost. At the time I was recovering from a catastrophic leg break, which you can read about later in the book. To understand fully what was about to unfold the experience turned my life upside down. The previous August I had smashed my tibia plateau in a fall while out running and spent months in recuperation. I had only just secured freelance work at Sky Sports News and felt my career was on the up. Unfortunately, not long after finding myself in the host's chair the accident happened.

I was determined to continue working there and wanted to show my commitment to the powers that be. A week after being discharged from hospital, I travelled down to London by car pumped full to the eyeballs with morphine and an Ilizarov cage wrapped round my lower right leg. I should never have been there, and my ambition ironically proved to be my downfall as the health and safety officer sent me home after a few weeks. Due to my injury I was forced to sell my cottage in Worsley and relocate to Wilmslow, a small well-to-do town just outside Manchester. I was devastated, but left with no choice as very little, if any, money was coming in. I had been working as a freelancer with many different broadcasters but being in a wheelchair for months on end meant I was unable to work. Thankfully, I made a very healthy profit after redeveloping the house and was able to relax for a while.

During this time, Setanta Sports secured the rights for the Scottish Premier League and I immediately informed them I was available for work. I arranged to meet their new head of production in Glasgow for lunch and to have a chat about the possibility of coming on board. He told me the company had plans for two brand-new club channels, Celtic and Rangers TV, and this is where he saw me fitting in. As much as I would be happy to look at this, I did tell him I had ambitions of presenting their SPL coverage.

It only took the head of production a few days to call me back and explain that he wanted to go with Rob MacLean as the main host of the SPL, which I completely understood and respected. He did, though, want to employ me, as the new face of Rangers TV. My heart sank! This was a serious dilemma. I was stuck between the proverbial rock and a hard place. I needed to get back to work and earn my crust. I wasn't exactly in the depths of deprivation but not far off, so the clock was well and truly ticking. I told the head of production I needed a few days to think about it, to talk it over with my friends and family. He told me the executive producer of the club channels would be in touch shortly to talk over the finer points.

I spoke with my Dad for hours as we weighed up the pros and cons. I spoke to people in the game, notably George Adams who was heading up the Rangers Youth Academy at the time who offered invaluable advice. By the time the executive producer called me and asked to meet in Glasgow, I was still to make my decision. The trip up the road from Manchester was a long one with my head full of thoughts and fears. My heart said "no" but my gut was saying, "you have no choice". By the time I met the powers that be in the old Scottish Television offices in Cowcaddens, I still needed convincing. This is when they told me they wanted me to host Celtic TV, and not Rangers. I could have hugged him but resisted. After going through the finer points of the contract I signed up there and then as the new face of Celtic TV. I immediately called my Dad and brother and could sense the relief in both their voices. Celtic we could handle, a great club with magnificent history and tradition and a stadium which, more importantly on a personal level, my late grandfather had frequented many times during his days as a football writer.

As an Aberdeen fan, I had no fears of presenting Celtic TV. There is, to a certain level, a degree of mutual respect between the two sets of fans but as in any society there is also the rivalry, be it healthy or not. I did not want to think about the negativity that could be generated amongst my fellow Aberdeen fans, or those of Celtic, but I knew bridges would have to be crossed and respect gained from the Celtic family. I was fully expecting a backlash from the Celtic fans after the press announcement. After all, here was an Aberdeen fan and former boy band member presenting their club's new TV channel.

The negativity came thick and fast! As is my way, my intention was to prove them wrong and shove their unflattering words right back down their throats. I knew it would take time and I was under no illusion that my style would not suit everybody. That goes with the territory, but I was determined to show I was worthy of the position. My boss asked me from the outset if being an Aberdeen fan would have an adverse effect on being the host and if my judgement at any time would be impaired. I reminded him quickly that I presented MUTV for five years while following Arsenal and was even in the chair the night Arsenal clinched the Premiership title at Old Trafford. My professionalism had never been called into question!

Celtic TV's flagship show was called the *Daily Huddle*, a Monday to Friday half-hour magazine show. The show's aim was to bring the very latest news from the club directly to the fans. The concept was simple but effective. On the show I was to bounce off the expert opinion of Jim Craig, a Lisbon Lion and Celtic legend. I had never met Jim before but knew of his reputation as a respected broadcaster and journalist who, to this day, remains the only professional footballer to qualify as a dentist. Jim and I hit it off immediately; he knew my grandfather well and enjoyed his company many times. I could not have asked for anyone better to help guide me during the early days. Jim's teachings of all things Celtic was invaluable, his stories were brilliant, and his knowledge of the game in Scotland outstanding. He wasn't just a source of strength in the early days – when the Celtic faithful were not exactly complimentary – but he and his lovely wife Elisabeth, or "Maw" as I like to call her, offered me the use of their home upon moving to Glasgow from Manchester.

I was waiting to sell my house in Manchester and move into my recently purchased apartment in the West End of Glasgow. In the interim period they very kindly put me up. Initially, I was only due to stay for three weeks... but I ended up staying for nearly three months! One of my more awkward moments while working for the channel came the night Aberdeen beat Celtic at Parkhead on October 27th 2004. The previous season, the Dons had managed to do what no other club had achieved in three years – beat Celtic on their home turf. So, in case history was to be repeated, I decided to attend the game on that cold October evening. After recording the *Daily Huddle* former Aberdeen striker Scott Booth, who was working as a reporter for Setanta, and I made arrangements to share a taxi to the ground from the office and watch the game from the relative comfort of the press box. Upon taking my seat there was some friendly banter flowing between myself and a group of fans behind me but I was conscious of being on my best behaviour.

It wasn't long before my manners were tested to the limit when the Dons found themselves two goals to the good in the opening minutes of the game. Scott and I simply patted each other on the knee in recognition of what was unfolding in front of our eyes while the masses around us looked on in disgust. Some people may find it difficult to understand why we weren't jumping up and down with the rest of the Red Army away to our right but Scott and I are professional and respectful enough to sit quietly and enjoy the moment without having to be over-exuberant. Plus, it's not really the done thing in a press box, not that that has stopped me before. I was once asked to take my seat by a steward at Rugby Park when my cousin Graham and I attended a game, which the Dons narrowly won 1–0.

Even though the Dons were winning 2–0, I was fully expecting an onslaught from Celtic and it wasn't long before the Hoops laid siege to David Preece's goal. Big Bobo Balde liked nothing more than a fierce challenge and needed no invitation to smash David into the post. David had to go off injured, Ryan Esson replacing him between the sticks. Scott and I pondered an early cup of tea and sandwich in the press room when the inevitable happened. John Hartson smashed home a low drive just before the break and the pendulum swung in Celtic's favour. It offered the home crowd the lift they were looking for and the air of anticipation rose as the second half kicked off. Aberdeen defended well and clung on to their slender advantage but with 20 minutes left Celtic were all square, John Hartson again being the man doing the damage as his fierce shot had too much power for Ryan Esson in the Dons' goal. Celtic Park erupted; I gently slumped in my seat already thinking of my post-match questions for Celtic manager Martin O'Neill. As the game came to a close I made my way down to the players' tunnel ready for the post- match interviews.

As I stood at the bottom of the stairs which led to the directors' box one of the stewards, whose job it was to guide the VIPs to their seats, motioned for me to join him and his colleague at the top of the stairs to watch the closing stages of the game. I politely rejected their offer as it was not my place to be up there but he was insistent. As I made my way up the steps I felt a surging pain in my bad knee and collapsed while clinging to the rail for dear life. The two stewards immediately sprang into action, grabbed me, helped me to my feet and offered me a helping hand into one of the comfortable chairs in the directors' box. As I took my seat, I felt eyes boring down on me from one of the club's PR representatives – a lady who shall remain nameless but one who was nothing but a pain in the arse the whole time I was there. Her levels of ignorance and pretentiousness reached heights that I never have, nor hope to experience again from any club employee. I sat in some discomfort while watching the final few moments of injury time when a long ball forward found Aberdeen striker John Stewart who glided past Bobo Balde and hit a low angled drive past goalkeeper David Marshall into the back of the Celtic net.

Seated directly in front of me in the directors' box was the official Aberdeen FC party, including legends Willie Miller and Jim Leighton. As the ball nestled in the back of the net they all jumped to their feet cheering wildly and exchanging high fives and hugs. I put my head down, clenched my fist and allowed myself a small smile at what was now undoubtedly a famous victory. The next morning at work as I joked

Top and above: Playing at Highbury

Right: Recovering at home after breaking my right leg, the extent of my injury meant bearing an Ilizarov Cage for three months – I would not recommend it!

My late father John Begg who this book is dedicated to.
Here he is a year before he passed, lost in his own thoughts, August 2006

Last pic of Dad and me, Christmas 2006

Enjoying a quiet moment inside Pittodrie Stadium, so many memories

A great moment in my life as an Aberdeen fan as I get my hands
on the Cup Winners' Cup – tempted to steal it! August 2011

Striking that now iconic Willie Miller pose!
Try and wipe that grin off my face

Getting ready for another busy *Daily Huddle* show on Celtic TV.
I spent three very happy years with 'the family'

My Celtic TV sparring partner, the legend that is Lisbon Lion Jim Craig!
The only professional football player to qualify as a dentist!!

Harley of Scotland knitwear photoshoot somewhere in the Highlands of Scotland 2008, a pout that would put Victoria Beckham to shame

At the Scottish League Cup Final with brother Peter and father-in-law Sigi

My beautiful family, Miriam and Lennox share a tender moment,
Doha 2014

Lennox and I watching Aberdeen

Aberdeen legend Alex McLeish and I in our
beIN Sports studios in Doha, Qatar

A sea of red, Scottish League Cup Final 2014

around with my Celtic-supporting colleagues I was dragged
into my boss's office. As I shifted uncomfortably in my chair
my boss explained that he had received a note from the very
same PR lady who had looked at me with such disdain saying
I should not under any circumstances be in the directors' box
and should always take my place in the press area. He went
on to say that she had complained about my behaviour saying
jumping up and down whilst cheering Aberdeen's winning
goal was not becoming of the presenter of the club's official
television station.

I told him quite sternly that I did not do such a thing and
would never behave in such an unprofessional manner and
resented the very accusation. My boss, to his credit, believed
me and simply told me to be more careful. My relationship
with that particular PR lady did not exactly bear fruit; I kept
out her way for the most part and, to be honest, felt better
for it. Thankfully, my professionalism was never questioned
again whenever Aberdeen and Celtic faced each other. On
the *Daily Huddle* it was not uncommon for the producers
to invite a guest to sit alongside Jim and have their say on
the day's topics. We had an array of guests over the years,
including nearly all the surviving Lisbon Lions. Bertie Auld,
who to this day remains the funniest man I have ever met,
and former Aberdeen and Celtic manager Billy McNeill, were
regular guests on the show.

Over the years I have shared many a laugh with my pundits
and guests on the variety of shows I presented for Granada
Shop, MUTV, Setanta and ESPN Star Sports in Singapore. I
believe I'm correct in saying that any presenter's nightmare is
to get a fit of giggles live on air. This has happened to me three
times. My first experience of "losing it" on air was during a
show I hosted with Andy Sheldon on Granada Shop. On that

particular Saturday morning, Andy and I were asked to host a 30-minute camping special, offering the viewer a host of products to help them along their merry way whilst out in the countryside! One of the products we had to sell was a rather large five-man tent. Now to explain Andy's personality; he is rather camp (excuse the pun) with a wicked sense of humour and needs no invitation to provide a laugh, be it appropriate or otherwise.

As we manoeuvred the tent into position, he asked me to unfold it, and in his very own unique camp manner, said to me; "Come on, dear boy, show me how big it is." Well, I almost buckled; thank the lord I was hidden from view by the tent as I fell about myself. I did my very best not to laugh out loud as I was fully aware of the audience, but I could not help it. As I hid from view trying to unfold the tent and contain my giggles, Andy did not help the situation by saying "where's he gone?"

As he realised what was happening, Andy started to guffaw. I could not look at him, as I knew if I caught his eye we would both be in big trouble. I'm just so grateful the tent was the last item we were selling and only had three minutes of airtime left. During those three minutes, I did not stop giggling even when Andy and I had to wrap up the show. He carried on like the consummate professional, and I, head in hands sniggered away, like a wee schoolchild.

One aspect of my job, which I am always meticulous about, is reading my scripts before going on air, but one night whilst hosting *The Red Hot News* on MUTV, I allowed my very high standards to slip. The news programme went to air three times a night, at 6.00pm, 8.30pm and a late bulletin at 10.00pm. The first two bulletins were pretty much the same but dependent on which producer was on duty, invariably the late bulletin had the odd change here and there. This particular evening I got caught up having a laugh with the gallery staff over dinner and didn't give myself enough time to prepare my scripts as we went to air at 10.00pm.

At the time, Sir Alex Ferguson was chasing a French left-back from Lille whose name, unfortunately, completely escapes me. I noticed from the show's run-down that I was to offer a small explanation to the viewer about the player and the reason why Sir Alex had moved his attentions elsewhere. What I wasn't ready for was the reason why the player was no longer on Sir Alex's radar! I began to read the autocue but soon found myself in the dreaded state of giggles. The player in question had been out for a walk with his dog, tripped over the said dog, bounced off a kerb and ruptured his ankle! I'm sorry the player injured himself but the circumstances sur-rounding the unfortunate event were enough to tip me over the edge and the hilarity began! I had images running through my mind of the lad falling over his dog and could not stop laughing but my problem – unlike at Granada Shop – was I had no tent to hide under, no co-host to take over, and still 15 minutes of the show to run!

I did my best to stop laughing but I couldn't. I was dying and I knew I still had two more reads to camera before I could throw to a feature. How was I going to get through the next couple of minutes or so, all in vision! I looked down, took a deep breath and tried to compose myself; it didn't work because as soon as I looked up into the camera I started laughing again! There was a deathly hush in my earpiece and I wondered if the gallery staff had all left the building. Thankfully, I managed to pull myself together for a few moments and carried on reading the autocue without any glitch. We went to a feature; I slumped over the desk and heard the gallery staff break into fits of laughter in my earpiece! The rest of the show went to plan without any added hiccups!

I'm quite ashamed to say I have been prone to the odd ricket here and there over the years. During the build-up to an important Premier League game between Arsenal and Manchester United on ESPN, I called Arsenal's Abou Diaby Abu Dhabi! It just so happened that joining me on the show that night were former Liverpool players Steve McMahon, Jason McAteer and Phil Babb, who needed no invitation to rip me apart for the rest of the evening! On a separate occasion I confused Tottenham's Gareth Bale with Batman actor Christian Bale and called a newspaper a spreadsheet instead of a broadsheet! The joys of live television!

As I mentioned before, Lisbon Lion Bertie Auld is one of the funniest characters I have ever met. Alongside Jim Craig, Billy McNeill and others, the *Daily Huddle*, at times, broke into choruses of laughter. One of our more popular shows on Celtic TV was the live phone-in show *Tic Talk* where the viewer was offered the chance to call in, speak to our guests and discuss a Celtic topic. One evening near Christmas 2006, I had to regain my composure like never before thanks to a certain Mr Auld, who that evening had Murdo MacLeod alongside him. The main topic up for discussion was Celtic's Japanese star Shunsuke Nakamura. "Naka", as he was fondly known, had recently expressed some feelings of homesickness. Many callers phoned in offering advice but one particular caller went a little too far with her idea. She suggested Naka should move back to Japan to be with his family and Celtic arrange for a private bus, very much like the ones you see rock stars tour in, to drive him back and forward from games. At first I believed the caller was "at it" and I had to ask her if she was being serious. She was adamant this was the best way forward for both club and player. Bertie and Murdo did their best not to laugh but quite obviously found the idea extremely amusing! This was the start of the downfall as both became a little giggly! I thanked the caller for her efforts and moved onto the next caller, a female who wanted to talk to Bertie. Bertie, in his own inimitable way, entertained the young lady for a couple of minutes with his patter. She was thrilled to be talking directly to a Celtic legend. Murdo was doing his best to contain his laughter from the caller before. I looked at him while the cameras focused on Bertie and whispered to him to behave himself while trying to contain my own amusement! It did not have the desired effect. Like before, I thanked the caller and gave the guys an opportunity to discuss more on the Naka subject. As Murdo offered his opinion, I noticed, out the corner of my eye, Bertie looking down at his trousers, licking his fingers and trying to clean away what appeared to be a small stain near his groin! This carried on for a few seconds.

Murdo also became aware of the rubbing and started to chuckle. The cameras zoomed out to a wide shot of the studio so all three of us were in vision. Bertie was oblivious as the licking and cleaning became a little more rigorous. I asked him if he was OK. He looked up realising he was now in vision and said; "Oh aye, I just got a wee bit carried away when talking to that lassie." I swear in that moment he rendered me speechless. Murdo began to slip off his chair in a fit of hysterics. Bertie was now chuckling away at his own joke. Through my earpiece, I could hear the gallery in fits of laughter while the camera of all places had to zoom in on me! I did my best not to laugh but it was a thankless task, the comment was so typical of Bertie that I just sat and giggled away. I daren't look eye-to-eye with Murdo as I knew he was gone; I looked at Bertie who tried to bring the conversation back to Naka but it was hopeless. I did my best to compose myself and silently prayed for my producer to go to a break but poor Craig was just as gone as everybody else. He managed to muster some sort of decipherable comment in my ear to throw to a break, which I was delighted to do.

When I knew we were in a break and out of harm's way, the laughter hit new levels. We had three minutes to get the laughter out of our systems before coming back live! I slumped back in my seat and let it all go, tears and all. Thankfully, the rest of the show bounced along just fine but it was difficult at times to meet each other's eyes in fear of the laughter starting all over again. Like most of my regular guests, I have kept in touch with Bertie and like nothing more on a stressful evening at work to take a moment, pick up the phone and natter on with him for a few minutes; he's the perfect de-stressing remedy!

One of the saddest days during my time at Celtic TV was the passing of the greatest of them all, Jimmy "Jinky" Johnstone. Jimmy succumbed to motor neurone disease and his untimely death was met with grief on a scale I have never witnessed before in the world of football. I was lucky enough to have met Jimmy once at a fund-raising event and his zest for life and determination were inspiring. He was quite obviously very ill as this awful disease ravaged his body to the point he could no longer hold up his head. His funeral was incredibly sad yet both Jim and Bertie had the strength to come on the *Daily Huddle* that very same evening for a two-hour phone-in special. It was undoubtedly the best two hours of television Celtic TV made as the stories of Jimmy flowed to the point we were all crying with laughter in the studio. After the show,

I hugged both Jim and Bertie as their emotions got the better of them. I don't know how they held it together as their best mate had just been laid to rest hours earlier and I will never forget their fortitude that night.

Tommy Burns' passing also left the Celtic family devastated. Tommy was a gentleman who was ready to greet all with a friendly smile. I adored him. In the early days he was always ready for advice and a natter. His influential words had a huge effect on me and helped me understand what Celtic Football Club, as an institution, meant to the fans and players. A particular favourite programme of mine was *The Green Room* where we invited ex-players to discuss their careers from childhood to the present day. It was the norm for the show to run for one hour; we had to ask Tommy back as he still had so much to tell. To fit his career into one hour proved an impossible task. It was obvious he loved Celtic and gave the club his all. I will never forget his anger after the Celtic under-19s were humiliated 5–0 by their Rangers counterparts in the Scottish Youth Cup Final. The very next morning the lads were dragged in early and given a lesson in what it meant to pull on the green and white hoops.

I asked him, nervously, if I could attend the training session at Barrowfield (Celtic's training ground) and he told me to bring the cameras and film the entire event. It was a coaching masterclass and I looked on in awe as this man handed down his expertise to these lads who only hours earlier felt the wrath of an embarrassed head of youth development. It made for a superb item on that evening's *Daily Huddle*. As much as he took his football and the development of his young stars very seriously, Tommy needed no invitation to have a laugh. Tommy was very quick to mock whenever Celtic beat the Dons, mostly in song!

I think he took particular enjoyment in watching me squirm. All in good jest, may I add. As much as he was ready to dish it out, he was ready to receive it back especially the night Aberdeen clawed back a two-goal deficit to draw 2–2 with the champions-elect at Pittodrie. Granted it was the last game of the season and meant little to Celtic, but the words "Stand Free" rang out the very next morning outside his office!

When my Dad died he was one of the first to call me and offer his condolences, his words will remain private but they gave me strength in what was an awful period in my life. Celtic Football Club, as a whole, offered me the type of kindness and compassion that left a lump in my throat when my Dad suddenly passed away on June 1st 2007. The club's chief executive Peter Lawwell arranged for two stunning bouquets to be delivered, one to Mum and one for Dad's grave. He penned a beautifully written letter to our family, which left me on the verge of tears. Neil Lennon personally called me, as did many of the players who left touching messages. I have nothing but the utmost respect for Neil Lennon. His will, determination and bravery is something I admire in the man. I hope he goes on to have a successful managerial career. In those dark days the kind words and support by, not just my colleagues at Setanta, but also all at Celtic FC, helped me through a horrific period. Even though the Dons will remain my number one love, my admiration and respect for Celtic is strong.

When I told Tommy Burns I was leaving Celtic TV he offered me a hug and wished me every success in the future. I was humbled when he left me a poignant video message alongside the coaching staff on my very last *Daily Huddle*. I kept in regular touch with Tommy right up until his death.

When his illness became aggressive I sent him a text message telling him I was thinking of him, to remain strong and that everybody loved him. Tommy died on May 15th 2008 and left a terrible void in so many lives. I watched his funeral from my office in Singapore and was unable to contain my own tears during Billy Stark's emotional speech. I have been very fortunate to meet many great people during my media career; Tommy is very high on that list.

As much as I enjoyed the company of all the guests over the years, I took a particular interest in those who had played for both Celtic and Aberdeen, notably, Derek Whyte, Joe Miller, Willie Falconer, Billy Stark and, of course, Gordon Strachan. As I mentioned before, I first met Derek when he was then the player-manager of Partick Thistle. He proved to be an excellent and valuable guest and we formed a strong friendship. Having worked for the BBC his understanding of television and how it works came in very useful.

Derek signed for the Dons when the club was in turmoil. Only weeks before, Roy Aitken had been sacked and Alex Miller took charge. I must confess that during this time I was a long-distance supporter of Aberdeen. Living and working in Hertfordshire meant, for many years, I was only able to follow the Dons from my armchair. Mind you, considering the form of the team during the late 1990s, some may argue this was not such a bad position to be in. In his four seasons with the club Derek played 131 games, many as captain.

Joe Miller was another whose company I enjoyed. Here was one of Aberdeen's finest youth products that, in his prime, was the target of many big clubs in England including Manchester United and Liverpool. Joe possessed a rare talent, which in the modern game is in danger of becoming extinct; like Messi and Ronaldo, he had the ability to run with the ball at his feet with devastating effect. Upon breaking into the first team in his late teens, Joe bamboozled opponents with his array of skills, quick feet and lightning turn of speed. Have Aberdeen had such a player since?

Willie Falconer also joined me on the odd occasion in the Celtic TV studio. I remembered him well from his playing days but Willie and I soon formed a friendship outside the studio, as he owned O'Brien's coffee shop on Byres Road in Glasgow. An establishment I frequented many times in the company of Derek Whyte for mocha, muffin and a natter. As well as managing the shop, Willie coached Motherwell's under-19 side and picking his brains at all things coaching helped me develop my own tactical understanding of the game in Scotland. This became very helpful in my role as host of the *Daily Huddle*. Willie was an interesting guest who offered the show a unique insight into youth football and how he believed the game should develop in Scotland. I'm sure many Aberdeen fans of my generation remember Willie's sweet left foot, which helped him notch 13 goals in his 77 games.

Unfortunately, my abiding memory of Willie in an Aberdeen shirt is one of my darkest as an Aberdeen fan, the 1987 Skol Cup Final against Rangers; the first time as a fan I did not attend a cup final. When the tickets went on general sale we were in Disneyland for the first time on a family holiday and missed out; I was devastated. Dad bled himself dry trying to obtain tickets for the game with the help of all my grandpa's connections but, alas, it was not meant to be. However, Willie has kindly offered to contribute to this book by telling me about that fateful day on October 25th 1987:

"I have so many memories from that final. Our first goal was a penalty from Jim Bett. I raced after a ball played over the top into the 18-yard box and found myself one-on-one with Nicky Walker. I remember thinking; 'Do I shoot first time, or take it round him?' Then I decided on the second option. I actually got past Nicky and was thinking to myself 'name in lights on the scoreboard, one nil!' Then the big Teuchter pulled me down. As any striker will tell you, I was gutted not to score but delighted when 'Jazzer' stroked it away.

"In all my years as a professional, this game was one of the best I've ever played in; the two teams attacked each other from the first whistle. With the score at 2–2, and about six or seven minutes left, the ball got crossed in from the right-hand side (I think it was Joe Miller or Jazzer). I made a run across Graham Roberts, managed to get a good contact on the ball with my head and – lucky for me – it flew into the top corner… Cue celebrations at the Aberdeen end (that feeling of scoring in a cup final for your home team club stays with you forever). Unfortunately, with only three or four minutes left on the clock, Robert Fleck scored to make it 3–3. Like every Dons fan, I thought that Willie Miller had been fouled in the build-up to the goal but the referee just waved play on. Some things never change!!

"So we went to penalties, for which we were not really prepared. Who was actually going to take the kicks had never been discussed before the game. Eventually, it came down to either Peter Nicholas, or me, for the last place of the five takers. Because Nico was older and more experienced than me at that time, he insisted it should be him. But, when he ran up and slammed his kick against the bar, I was thinking that I might have been the better option!

"We all felt sorry for Nico, who was a great guy in the dressing room; he was just the unlucky one that day. After the match we travelled back up the road, and had a few drinks on the bus; it should have been a miserable trip back home but the great team spirit we had at the club at that time showed through and we just felt determined to do better next time."

Another guest on the programme was Billy Stark, a man whose friendship, compassion and ultimate generosity will stay with me for many a day. He signed from St Mirren in 1983 and a year later had the unenviable task of filling Gordon Strachan's boots when the wee man left for Manchester United. His former team-mates have nothing but good words about their former colleague, who worked tirelessly for the cause. Billy was liked by all and was one of the more popular characters in the dressing room in the mid 1980s. I will remember Billy for his driving runs into the final third of the pitch to support the front men, his superb heading technique from corners or free kicks, which offered the Dons many an important goal. His contribution to Aberdeen's success should not be underestimated.

I first met Billy as a young starry-eyed boy outside Hampden in the immediate aftermath of the Dons lifting the 1986 Scottish Cup. As the players made their way onto the team bus I asked Billy for his autograph to add to those of Jim Leighton and Neil Simpson. He obliged immediately. That programme remains at home safely hidden away from prying eyes. Fast forward many years and my producer at Celtic TV, Craig Coughlan, asked me if I thought Billy Stark would make a good guest on our show. I called my uncle Bill who told me having Billy on the show was a fabulous idea. Unknown to me at that time, Billy and my uncle were firm friends. Billy swept into our office the very next day and I admit I was a tad nervous meeting him; here standing in front of me shaking my hand was a man who was one of my childhood heroes.

Over the coming months Billy was a regular, his immaculate manner, articulate speech and brilliant knowledge, in my opinion, gave us the edge over our rivals on Rangers TV. Without blowing smoke up the backsides of all that worked on Celtic TV, we blew Rangers TV's daily show out of the water. Billy liked to come in early for a coffee and a chat – the Dons being the main topic for discussion. I loved picking his brains, listening to his stories and soaking up his knowledge. It was not uncommon for my cousin Graham, my uncle and I to have an afternoon at Hampden to watch Billy's Queen's Park. The only time I did not talk to Billy was when his Queen's Park side knocked the Dons out the CIS Insurance Cup at Firhill after a penalty shoot-out! That night, the Dons were simply awful; no desire, no commitment and no will to win. Queen's deserved to go through and I congratulated Billy on his finest hour, albeit through gritted teeth!

Billy was always willing to share a story and answer my questions about his time at the Dons. I think he understood my passion for Aberdeen and my obvious enthusiasm and this was reflected in a gesture that, to this day, I still have to pinch myself to believe actually happened. As he walked into the studio carrying a Marks & Spencer's shopping bag I jokingly said; "Doing your messages for Mrs Stark are we?" He offered the bag and told me to look inside. Opening the bag I looked at what appeared to be a tracksuit, a red one.

Billy motioned for me to take it out the bag, which I did. Upon unfolding the said tracksuit I gazed in wonder at what I was holding. Here in my hands was the official Aberdeen

Football Club tracksuit from the 1983 Cup Winners' Cup Final! Billy said "that's for you". For a few seconds I could not quite believe it. I honestly had no idea what to say; I looked up at him as he smiled back and I very humbly said I could not accept this extraordinary gift. I said to him that he deserved this more than I did but he stopped me in my tracks and told me that Sir Alex Ferguson had given it to him when he joined the club to make him feel part of the family and the success Aberdeen were having at that time.

Billy continued to tell me that the tracksuit was only collecting dust in his loft and he would rather it go to someone who would treasure it, hence why he gave it to me. All I could do in that moment was hug him; it was an astonishingly kind gesture for which I am extremely grateful. Apart from my wife Miriam and baby son Lennox, that tracksuit is my most treasured possession. I continually have to pinch myself that I own such an important artefact from Aberdeen's history. Billy's generosity that day left me on the verge of tears, he must have known what having such an item means to me and for that act alone he will always have a part to play in my life. We talk regularly and I'm thrilled his coaching skills are now being put to good use at the very highest level. Billy Stark, I salute you!

In my three years in Glasgow many Celtic fans asked me what Martin O'Neill was like? Martin was Celtic manager and hero to thousands when I joined Setanta in the summer of 2004. I knew Martin's assistant Steve Walford as I used to play football with him during my years with the Arsenal Charity team, so I had ideas of using Steve to get to know Martin. This task proved fruitless, as Martin unfortunately did not want to get to know me. Fair enough. But I would have thought that as the club's official TV station, he might have been more understanding of what we were trying to achieve. I believe he saw us as just another media outlet. To be fair to Martin, in hindsight I believe the powers that be at Setanta should have done more to explain what the role of the channel was, and where its place within the Celtic media sat.

It was down to the executive producer and I to arrange a meeting with Mr O'Neill and discuss what hopes and dreams we had for the channel, and how we hoped he would play an integral part in its success. Mr O'Neill listened intently while my boss set out our agenda but he offered little back; I believe to this day he wanted little or nothing to do with us. I liked him, I found him interesting yet mysterious and wish I had the opportunity to interview him on more than the odd occasion he gave up his time for us. In the 12 months I knew him he sat down with us for a one-on-one interview only twice. He did, though, allow us to talk to him about his own career; it was fascinating stuff and I only wished we had had more time with him. Alas, it was not meant to be. This brings me nicely to one of the reasons why I believe Mr O'Neill kept us at arm's length, a certain Mr Dominik Diamond and his now infamous appearance on the *Daily Huddle*.

Ahead of that particular show, a debate raged in the office as to whether Dom should appear at all. My executive producer was in Dom's corner but the show's producers vehemently fought against having him appear as a guest as they believed his unflattering opinions could damage the relations between club and TV channel. I played devil's advocate, sat back and watched with interest as to who would win this particular argument. Frankly, there was never any doubt as to the outcome; the executive producer is the boss, it's his call and on his head befalls the consequences. Twenty-four hours later he was reaping what he had sowed!

Dom is well known for his outrageous style, his unique delivery of all things topical and is never shy of offering an opinion or three. Every morning as I walked to work from my apartment in the West End, I listed to his breakfast show on "Beat 106". It was by far the best show of all in the Central belt. As we took our seats in the studio, Jim Craig and Dom chatted on and I could see an instant connection. I had a good feeling about the show. I did my introductions, welcomed the viewers, did the usual greetings to my guests and delivered my opening question to Dom. I asked him for his thoughts on the season so far and his hopes from now until the end of the current campaign. I was not primed for his response.

His opening line went something like this; "If Celtic don't win the league at the end of the season, Martin O'Neill should be sacked; in fact he should be sacked for not playing Aiden McGeady every week." I took a deep breath; Jim's jaw hit the desk. Dom continued; "Alan Thompson and Rab Douglas should never play for the club again." There was a stunned silence from the gallery. Normally, you get constant feedback in the earpiece but that night not a peep was heard from my producer, as I believe he fell off his chair. I thought quietly to myself that the shit was about to hit the fan! I had to think fast and try and divert the attention away from Dom so looked to Jim for help; thankfully, he jumped in and argued Dom's point.

Dom was very comfortable talking about what obviously was his passion; he did not hold back, a fans' fan! Contentious comment after contentious comment, without taking breath, flowed from his mouth, which did little to soothe my producer's nerves. But, as I sat and watched on, I could not help but think that what I was witnessing was great television. It was quite a contrast. A Lisbon Lion and Celtic legend, who played the game at the very highest level, and an outspoken fan who is only voicing what he honestly believes. I kept quiet and let them get on with it. As the show moved merrily along Dom continued to present valid arguments and I was captivated by the brilliance of both men in the short time we had together. At the end of the show I thanked them for a fascinating insight from two fervent and passionate supporters, albeit from different angles. I walked out the studio knowing I was in deep shit with the club but elated at the quality of the programme we had just aired. I asked Dom to grab a seat in the canteen and I would be with him shortly.

As Jim and I waited in the vast corridor outside Studio A, he was in no doubt that we were in big trouble; I agreed. My producer Craig Coughlan walked towards us, tapes in hand looking slightly the worse for wear. In his usual comical way he looked at us both, shrugged his shoulders, said "oh well" and burst out laughing. Craig lightened the mood further still by saying; "Don't worry lads, nae fucker is watching anyway."

As was my way, I left the guys to walk the short distance back to the office while I made my way back to the canteen. I thanked Dom for a brilliant show but told him I doubt we would see him on Celtic TV again. My hunch proved correct as Dom unfortunately was banned by the powers that be at the club. A real shame in my opinion, as he was the type of guest we needed; colourful, insightful, educated and funny. I understood why Celtic made their decision; at the end of the day we were the club's official TV channel, therefore accountable to the club. They had editorial rights over us and watched on like hawks. We, as the production team, had a duty to protect and deliver, but with my experience at MUTV I knew there was a very fine line between safeguarding the players, manager and coaches and insulting the intelligence of the fans.

The fans pay their money to see the team, they paid their subscription fees to Setanta to have Celtic TV, and they as supporters are entitled to their own opinion. Fans are not stupid, fans are fully aware when the wool is being pulled over their eyes. On the odd occasion – and I cannot stress enough that it was only now and then – we were guilty of blinding the fans. Banning Dom was one of those times.

The day after the night before I was due at Celtic Park to interview John Hartson, a lovely guy whose company I enjoyed every time we met. I was nervous as I made my way to the ground in a taxi. Upon arrival, Celtic's elderly doormen John and John greeted me in their usual way and proceeded to shake their heads in tandem and tut rather loudly. This did nothing for my nerves. I could feel the tension as I sat down and waited for the PR person to turn up. I was so nervous that I eventually kept myself occupied by holding the door open as the players made their way into the ground and offering a sheepish "good morning" to most.

I suddenly found myself thinking why was I behaving like this? I had done nothing wrong, I had only loaded the gun; Dominik Diamond had well and truly fired it, scoring maximum points in my humble opinion. Big Rab Douglas appeared. I said "good morning" and without a blink or hint of acknowledgement he walked straight past me. Then Alan Thompson and Chris Sutton arrived in tandem as they did most mornings. Thompson scowled at me as I bid both a friendly "good morning"; Sutton in his usual smug way looked straight ahead as though I was not good enough to keep his company.

Thankfully, Mr O'Neill's assistant John Robertson soon followed and took me to one side and said; "The gaffer is not happy with what was said on Celtic TV last night but don't worry too much son as it will soon blow over." All of a sudden I felt very much in the firing line. I have no idea what went on behind the scenes at Celtic Park after that show, and frankly it's absolutely none of my business, but I believe damage was done and bridges had to be built. The small Celtic TV team did their utmost to rebuild those bridges and did a marvellous job doing so, a task in my opinion which went unnoticed by the bigwigs in their ivory towers at Setanta.

Mr O'Neill kept his distance from us from that day forward. As I said before, I wish I could have got to know him better but I have nothing but the utmost respect for him especially considering the difficult period he was having in his personal life. He is a fantastic man manager and coach.

Which brings me nicely to Gordon Strachan. When Mr O'Neill announced he was leaving Celtic we all wondered who would be the new gaffer? So many names were thrown into the hat that it all became very exciting. Mr O'Neill and the Celtic board called a press conference where he would address the gathered media for the last time and chief executive Peter Lawwell would name the new manager of Celtic. As the hordes of journalists and cameras fought for space within the boardroom and the name of Gordon Strachan left the lips of Celtic's chief executive, I could not help but smile! Here was one of my all-time heroes about to step through the corridors of Celtic Park and take over the reins of this huge club. I could not wait!

Gordon first attracted my attention as a youngster during the Uefa Cup tie against Ipswich Town at Pittodrie in 1981. His performance that night was outstanding, winning and blasting home the penalty to open the scoring, gliding in and out of the classy Ipswich midfield and showing his true class against a side who were dominating the old English First

Division at the time. Alongside Peter Weir, they both tore Bobby Robson's side apart. The only blot that night was a missed penalty right at the death but it mattered little. The Dons had knocked the holders out and made the rest of the country sit up and take notice. I marvelled at his display and can remember going over all the newspapers the following day with Dad, who was just as impressed.

Gordon is completely unaware of this, but I first met him when Dad took me to a midweek game four days after my tenth birthday on August 25th 1982, when the Dons entertained Morton in the League Cup. Dad had been especially invited to Pittodrie by the commercial department. I was overcome with excitement as this was my first chance as a fan to get up close and personal with my new-found heroes. I had been a fan for a year, watched the Dons lift the Scottish Cup only months before, and was now a well and truly devoted dandy.

We took our seats in what is now the Gothenburg suite at Pittodrie and enjoyed the plush surroundings. Our seats in the main stand gave us the perfect view of the action. I have little recollection of the game but will never forget what happened after the match. Little did I know, the players always paid a visit to the club's guests after the game and spent time with those lucky enough to find themselves in such a privileged position. As I munched on another biscuit Alex Ferguson walked into the room. He walked straight over, shook Dad's hand and I listened on as the two of them became engrossed in a conversation about grandpa. This was brilliant! Alex occasionally looked down on me, patted my head and smiled; this was so cool! As he said his goodbyes he shook my hand, grabbed my matchday programme, signed it and said "see you soon, son". As I stared at the autograph in disbelief big Doug Rougvie was the next to make an appearance. He came over and said "hello" as he towered above me, signed my programme, then went on his merry way. John Hewitt was next, quickly followed by Mark McGhee, whose signature dominated the front cover; I was in heaven and loving every minute of it. Gordon Strachan was the last player to say hello. He came over, shook my hand, and asked Dad if all was OK and if we had enjoyed the match? I thrust a pen in his hand and asked him for his autograph. He laughed and signed below all the others. That programme, like so many others, is a prized possession; it's a trip back to the very early days, those great days when the Dons were just about to embark on something very special.

For the next two seasons Gordon became a firm favourite, a gifted midfielder who epitomised everything the Dons were about in the early 1980s. I noticed, as I started to attend away games, that Gordon was the target of much abuse from opposition fans. His teammates, though, were always quick to protect a player they obviously had a huge amount of respect for. I'm sure, like so many other fans of my generation, they have endless memories of Gordon. The ingenious free-kick with John McMaster against Bayern Munich; his goal against Rangers in the 1982 Scottish Cup Final, and the subsequent comical forward roll with that little trickle of blood coming out his nose. His coolness every time he stepped up to take a penalty and my personal favourite, the look on his face as he turned away to celebrate John Hewitt's winner against Bayern Munich at Pittodrie. I implore you to watch it, again and again; it's nothing short of brilliant. If you don't get goosebumps watching that particular clip then I dare to question your passion!

When it was announced he was leaving the Dons for Manchester United after the 1984 Scottish Cup Final I was devastated. I was also confused and struggled to understand why anybody would want to leave Aberdeen? As I read the headline report in the *P&J*, I asked Dad if they had made a mistake, was he really leaving? Dad seemed just as disappointed. The news flattened me and I went to school that morning feeling deflated. I followed Gordon's career from there on in as he made the natural step into management.

When he was announced as Celtic manager, I wondered how long it would take for me to build a relationship with him. I didn't have to wait long. My first meeting with Gordon was the day after his first press conference. We had agreed to meet in his office at Celtic Park at 9am the following day. I sat, slightly nervous, in the reception area – while waiting for him – going through in my own mind what I would say to him. As he walked through the big glass doors at precisely 9am, he said; "Give me five minutes Ally." I was shocked he knew my name. Did he know me? When I think about it, I realised that the answer had to be "yes".

When he agreed to take over the reins from Martin O'Neill, surely he dipped into Celtic TV to see what we were all about? My hunch proved correct when I was led into his office. He told me he had watched the *Daily Huddle* on the odd occasion and enjoyed the show. He even made me laugh by saying he was a sad individual with nothing better to do than watch Celtic TV! For the next few minutes I explained what the aim of the channel was and how I hoped he would play his role. Eventually, he agreed to be interviewed every Friday morning at 9am to discuss various topics. I was elated! After the formalities, I confess I told him I was a big Aberdeen fan and he was one of my childhood heroes, which I think he found quite amusing. I gave him my word that my professionalism would never be questioned and to use the channel as a platform to speak, if he so wished. I thanked him for his precious time, wished him the very best of luck and told him I had every faith he would have a very successful period as manager of Celtic Football Club.

I sensed he would do well but I did not imagine for one minute the impact he would have on the club in the next four years as there were many doubters, especially amongst the fans. This is just a personal opinion but I believe they were very much divided; some simply did not accept him, a notion, to this day, I still can't get my head around. Obviously, he got off to the worst possible start after being soundly beaten by Artmedia Bratislava but, to his credit, he was still very much willing to sit down on the Friday morning and discuss the match in detail. I chose my questions carefully with the help of my producer Craig. We needed to find out, from him, what went wrong without pissing him off.

I always went through my questions with Gordon before the interview so he understood 100% what we were trying to get at. In all my time with him he refused, only once, to answer a question. He was a joy to sit down with, always ready for a laugh and giving up his time ahead of training. His football brain is outstanding, his knowledge frightening, and it all added to what, for the most part, were interesting and intriguing interviews. He allowed our cameras to attend training if we asked beforehand. If an unsavoury incident happened in training – which on more than one occasion it did and we caught it – he would ask us to make sure it was not for public use. We obliged. On many occasions I would try and engage him in talk about his time with Aberdeen ahead of an interview to warm him up while the cameraman prepared.

He would chat now and then about that time but I learnt quickly that Gordon is not one for talking about himself, or his career. I did not force the issue but I believe he understood my passion for the club and on the odd occasion would chuck in a story or two. I loved it; it was a time tunnel back to my youth and all those great days spent at Pittodrie watching him. I was delighted for him when he won the SPL championship in his first year, proving the doubters wrong. When he took Celtic into the last 16 of the Champions League it was an astonishing achievement, yet the doubters were still not convinced. I sometimes wonder if these fans believe they have the divine right to win everything. I would give my left arm for Aberdeen to challenge for the title, win the Scottish or League Cup and compete in the Champions League. Like me, I'm sure all Aberdeen fans want us to play in the Champions League against the likes of Barcelona, AC Milan and Manchester United. Under Gordon Strachan, Celtic did and gave the Parkhead faithful some incredible nights filled with drama. We obviously came close with the marvellous Europa League campaign of season 2007/08 when Pittodrie once again tasted European glory but the Champions League, I believe, is a stretch too far.

I spoke to Gordon the day after they beat Hearts to win the top division and, as you can imagine, he was quietly delighted. He took it all in his stride as he knew he would have to keep delivering; that's what the fans expect! I was so happy for him and his coaching staff. He continued to deliver. Yes, there were blips along the way and at times Celtic Park seemed like a revolving door with the amount of players coming and going. He built a new team, one that won the league title three seasons in a row, the first time that had happened since the days of Jock Stein, but still some fans weren't happy.

Some may argue those particular fans have been spoilt. I say try being an Aberdeen fan for the past 25 years then those that continued to dislike Gordon may begin to understand that, in fact, having him as their club manager is not such a bad thing after all. When ESPN came calling in May 2007, I asked Gordon for his advice; he told me to take the job, as the opportunity was too good to turn down. He told me that working at Setanta and the club channel had put me in good stead for bigger and better things but after more than three years the time was right to move on. He was one of only a few whose advice I went looking for, the others being my Dad, my brother and my good friend Campbell Gray. The day I left Celtic Park for the last time Gordon took me aside, wished me well and told me to continue my good work and that he would always be available if I needed him, a gesture which touched me. We have kept in touch and he has kept his promise; he is not just a true legend in my opinion, he is in every way a true gentleman.

During my time with Celtic TV we rarely had disappointing days, frustrating days, yes, but disappointing – not so much. One such day actually turned out to be quite surreal. I was seated at my desk in the Setanta office busy writing my script for the *Daily Huddle* when my office phone rang. I picked up, said "hello", and took a second to wonder if someone was playing a joke. On the other end of the line was Hollywood movie actor and passionate Celtic fan James McAvoy.

James had recently performed (quite brilliantly, may I add) in the Hollywood movie *Last King of Scotland* with Forest Whitaker, a sensational film that I rarely tire of watching. James had called to ask me for my help in acquiring a number of Celtic football strips for a trip he was to make to Uganda for a documentary being made by the Discovery Channel. I was delighted to be given the opportunity to help. I asked him to leave it with me and I would see what I could do; in return he would make every effort to appear on the *Daily Huddle*, or do a sit-down interview with me. It turned out he subscribed to Celtic TV and was an avid watcher of the show.

Over the next few days I pestered Suzanne Reid at the club – who works in the merchandising division – for a number of replica strips, of varying sizes, to be shipped to James at his London home ahead of his trip to Africa. Suzanne could not have been more helpful and duly obliged with a number of brand new strips for the kids in the village James was due to visit. I kept him up to speed with my progress and was delighted to report, after a few days, a number of kits were obtained and packed up ready to be sent. He seemed genuinely delighted! A tick in the box, I thought, and allowed myself a wee smile on a job well done.

However, and most annoyingly, once the package had been sent I did not hear from James again. After a couple of weeks I put in the odd call but was very aware of his busy filming schedule and became painfully mindful of disturbing him so I tried another route, his PR representative. Who was I kidding? After the odd email or five I gave up; I felt a tad betrayed and used, but hey ho! That's life. His PR representative was as much use as I am to the world of computer mathematics but as Justin Timberlake once said, "What goes around, come around." I would like to thank James and his power-tripping PR rep for providing me with another anecdote for my book.

In a recent interview I was asked for my fondest memory from my days at Celtic TV, I have many but one particular programme sticks out. On the 37th anniversary of Celtic winning the European Cup the producers put forward a plan to hold a two-hour *Daily Huddle* special to commemorate the occasion. It was decided Billy McNeill and Bertie Auld would join Jim in the studio with Jimmy Johnstone joining us on the phone from his home. To mark this one-off show I asked the powers that be at Celtic if we could borrow the replica European Cup for the show. I was given permission under one very important condition, that I take sole responsibility for the trophy from the moment it left Parkhead to the second I brought it back. The importance of this task obviously had to be taken very seriously so I agreed and told my producers of my plan!

The day of the show I drove to Celtic Park, picked the trophy up, and placed it carefully in the well of the front passenger seat of my car. As I drove back to the office I jumped on the M8 motorway thinking it was the quickest way back, until I hit a traffic jam. The look on the faces of some bus and lorry drivers is something that will stay with me for a long time. The comical double-takes and profound confusion was as hilarious as I have ever seen. I must admit, I did wonder if at any given moment I would be pulled over by the police and asked to explain what I was doing with the European Cup! Thankfully, I didn't and the trophy was delivered without incident.

The actual show itself was nothing short of magical as we reminisced about that famous day in Lisbon all those years ago. As I sat back and marvelled at the brilliance, I could see the joy in the faces of these three legends as they took a trip down memory lane. My job for two hours was to ask the odd question but to be honest my presence was not needed as the boys took over. Here I was in the company of three Lisbon Lions, I felt privileged, honoured and very proud that these guys all became close friends. I loved that evening, it's why I do the job that I do.

I spent three very happy years working for Setanta Sports and Celtic TV; I forged strong friendships and continued to learn my trade. I feel quite blessed to have been accepted by the majority of the Celtic family. In particular, fans' website The Huddleboard, who openly criticised me in the early days, became a firm supporter of mine, as did others, and I continue to enjoy the banter with those on "te borad" to this day. Glasgow is a fantastic city, a reformed city. It's like someone has opened a window to let the light in – the city glistens, even sparkles! Very much like Aberdeen, Glasgow is in my blood. It will remain very close to my heart until the day I hope to walk her paths again.

Break a leg

On August 19th 2003, my life was turned upside down. At the time I lived in Worsley, Manchester. As was my way back then, I kept myself very fit, running most nights, playing football and the occasional game of golf. This particular night I decided to take a night off as I wanted to watch football on TV, but my ex persuaded me to come for a quick run. It was a decision I have regretted ever since! We set off through Worsley woods on the same route we did most nights. As we turned the last corner, with our 500-year-old cottage in sight I decided to up the pace. Ahead of me was a mound of sand. For those of you who are old enough to remember *Junior Kick-Start* – a cross bike challenge on BBC many years ago – you will know exactly what I mean. For those of you who are not, bear with me!

As I sprinted away from my ex, I pretended to be a bike in *Junior Kick-Start*, making the noises and revving an imaginary throttle with my hand. I had ideas of running up the sand, doing an elaborate star jump, and landing safely on the other side of the mound. It went horribly wrong! As I ran up the sand and jumped I realised quickly I had jumped high and long. Frankly, I panicked, lost my balance and came down heavily on the path. As I landed, I felt as if I had been hit with a sledgehammer across the side of my right knee. There was a thud, no pain, but yet I knew instantly I had done some damage!

As I rolled over to my left to support my leg, my ex came running over and in a panicked state said; "Oh God, you've broken your leg." "No," I replied, "It's OK, I've damaged my bloody knee." She told me to look down: I was not ready for what I saw. Just below my kneecap, to the side of my leg, the bone was sticking through the skin! Then suddenly the pain hit me and I screamed in agony!

I cannot begin to explain the enormity of the pain. I had broken bones before; my foot, my wrist and my nose – all playing football – and my left index finger when I tried to punch a member of pop group Worlds Apart during a basketball feature for a pop magazine. I can't remember the dude's name as this particular boy band changed their line-up so many times I never knew who was who. What I do remember was that he tried to sneakily elbow my bandmate David during a passing movement and I saw red, steamed in, grabbed him, punched him across the top of his skull as he ducked and broke my bloody finger!

That was painful but it was nothing compared to what I was enduring while lying on the path in Worsley woods. To cut a horrible story short, I lay in a hospital bed for a month and had an Ilizarov cage bolted to my right leg for three months. As I lay at home recovering, I became acutely aware that I was unable to bend my right knee. It felt very stiff and it was incredibly painful. As I studied my X-rays I noticed, to my horror, that my knee was free of the bolts, which I was under the impression, were preventing me from bending my knee. I had assumed my knee had a bolt through it; in fact, it did not! I panicked, thinking something was very much wrong. I called my good friend, Blackburn Rovers physiotherapist Dave Fevre, and asked him if he would be so kind to pop round and have a look. At this time I have to explain that my thinking, judgement and decision making was very much impaired thanks to the very strong morphine tablets I was taking for the pain.

Dave took one look at me, said I was in big trouble and he would try and arrange physiotherapy for me at the club immediately. Physio was on offer from the hospital but it was a complete waste of time. During my stay I was put on an isokinetic machine, which basically bends my knee for me. But as my knee had grown stiff it became an extremely difficult and unpleasant procedure. The physios in hospital were so busy with other patients, that they had little time for someone they deemed fit and able. I have no complaints over this as young children and the elderly rightfully take preference, but I was in a bad way and would have appreciated more than five minutes of their time to tell me to continue doing my exercises, which were clearly not working!

Dave told me he would have to get permission from Blackburn's club doctor and the manager at the time, Graeme Souness. He called Mr Souness on his mobile, explained the situation and hung up with a smile; Mr Souness had no problems with Dave treating me. The very next day I was driven to Blackburn Rovers' training ground and began what I always remember as the most pain-filled hour of my life. The first task Dave had on his hands was to unglue my kneecap. Without going into the gory details, due to the severity of my break, blood had spilled into the knee cavity. When my knee fell back into place, it went straight on top of the blood, the blood formed scar tissue, took a hold of my knee and dragged it down; that was why I was unable to bend my knee!

He laid me on the bed, making sure the Ilizarov cage was secure, and took a hold of my right knee in the palms of his hand. He told me to brace myself and warned that this was not going to be pleasant. He started to physically move my knee back and forward from right to left. I cried out in pain; it was horrific! I tried to grab his hand but he brushed me aside as his assistant took a hold of me and almost pinned my arms together. Dave continued. By now I was doing my best not to cry out in anguish but it was impossible.

My arms stiffened up around my chest as the pain became too much. I couldn't breathe. Dave stopped. I slumped back gasping for air, my head spinning, and my skin sweating. I begged him not to do it again but for my own sake he had no choice, so round two started! I cried out again, shocked at the severity of the pain. By this time I was becoming acutely aware of people gathering in the doorway leading to the gym; it was the players. I could see them all staring in disbelief at my metalwork. I tried to hide my face but I couldn't move my arms. I looked away almost embarrassed. Dave and his assistants did their best to make me comfortable, helping me breathe, holding me while he worked away on my knee. As I tried to lie back I noticed a figure hanging over me. I was having problems focusing properly as the pain intensified but when I looked up, Graeme Souness was looking down on me! Graeme Souness! A man, that during my teenage years, I had grown to hate. He was the enemy, the epitome of everything that I disliked about football, and Rangers, at the time.

Graeme looked concerned, almost shocked. He put his hand on my shoulder and told me to hang on in there. He looked at Dave for some sort of reasoning but Dave was too busy concentrating on my knee. After what felt like an eternity, he stopped and said that was enough for the moment. Graeme did not move from my side for 15 minutes. After Dave finished with my knee he turned me over, again making sure my metalwork was secure and continued his work, stretching, pulling and massaging! I was ready to pass out. During the whole process, Graeme did not move from my side and continued to offer me words of encouragement.

For the next six months I was allowed to attend physiotherapy at the football club without anyone asking any questions. The process was slow, at times incredibly frustrating, as my knee played hard to get. Dave set a target of 90 degrees flexion, which we achieved with much hard work, but it was obvious more surgery was required. Scar tissue had formed around the joint and it came to a point where this restricted all movement. The only way to allow more movement was for the scar tissue to be removed, hence the requirement for more surgery.

I would like to thank Mr Souness for allowing me the use of the medical facilities and the expert help of Dave who has now become one of my closest friends. I owe them a huge debt of gratitude. Isn't it funny how, as kids, you deplore somebody because you see their face on television or kicking lumps out of your heroes, yet as an adult Mr Souness to me is nothing but a gentleman whose kindness and words helped me through some awful pain-stricken hours. After I made the move to Glasgow, my knee deteriorated to the point I was struggling to walk. One morning whilst at Celtic Park I was hobbling through the players' area when the club doctor Roddy McDonald asked me what was wrong; I briefly explained. Roddy asked me into his office to have a closer look. Upon stripping off and lying on the medical table, Roddy's face told a thousand words. He asked me if this is how I was left nearly 18 months after the initial accident.

When I said "yes", I believe he was a little shocked. As he prodded and poked around my joint it was obvious Roddy knew I was in a bad way. He asked me for my medical records including all reports and X-rays, which I supplied the next day. Like before he was utterly shocked when he saw my fracture for the first time. At this point the club's physio Tim Williamson made an appearance and I think Tim was just as perplexed. A plan was put in place! Over the next few days or so, Roddy made some calls and it was arranged for me to attend the Southern General Hospital on the south side of the river Clyde to meet renowned knee surgeon, Colin Walker. Our first meeting was brief but very productive. Mr Walker explained that I required more extensive surgery to remove scar tissue from both the back and front of the knee joint.

Upon this an extensive rehabilitation programme was put in place. I would attend the hospital twice a week for physio and Roddy organised for me to attend the Celtic gym twice a week with Graham Parsons, the reserve team physio. Basically, for the next few weeks I would have physiotherapy nearly every day! Gordon Strachan gave his kind permission for me to use the gym as long as the physios' work was done with the players and the gym was quiet. I couldn't wait to get started!

Two to three weeks passed before Mr Walker could fit me in to his already packed schedule. I must admit, as I was lying on the bed waiting for the anaesthetist to knock me out, I felt a tad nervous at what lay ahead. All I was hoping for was more movement and pain relief; I had lived with constant pain for going on two years. For those who have never been under the knife, waking from surgery is an odd experience. I was aware somebody was slapping my face and calling my name. I could see them but they were at the end of what felt like a long tunnel. Before I knew it, I was at the end of the tunnel and the voice and the slapping became more prominent. I was awake!

I looked at my knee and what stared back was like something from a Frankenstein movie. My knee was gone, replaced by a mound of skin, all different colours and staples, from the bottom of my thigh to the top of my shin. It looked horrible and I fell back feeling the pain for the first time. Thank God for morphine, I thought, as I took a deep dose and immediately feel into a dream state. Upon waking again, this time in the ward, I was aware my leg was moving, but I wasn't moving it. As I looked down I could see my leg was strapped into an isokinetic machine. It's a fantastic contraption with which settings can be adjusted depending on the flexion and pain tolerance. I was strapped in for the next 48 hours!

I lay in hospital for the next three days and only once Mr Walker was satisfied that the surgery wounds were healing, and my knee had sufficient movement, did he allow me home. Then the hard work had to start all over again. Roddy at Celtic arranged for me to attend physio the very next day. Graham took a hold of me and started working on bending my knee. As the staples restricted the movement, he did what he could to manipulate the area, not the most pleasant of experiences. In fact, a swift kick to the bollocks may have been more pleasurable!

I spent the good part of an hour being prodded, pulled, rubbed and jolted as Graham worked his magic. After a few days I attended the hospital for a check-up and Mr Walker was satisfied enough to remove the staples from the long incision down my knee. It was another less-than-pleasant moment. The nurse – who I have to say looked slightly sadistic – unnerved me; I think she was looking forward to this. To remove the staples, she cut them with a pair of what looked like garden pliers and pulled them through my leg one by one. Unfortunately, there were 30 of the little buggers! As I yelped once or twice she looked up at me and told me in a very brogue Glaswegian accent to "behave myself"; I quietly apologised for acting slightly cowardly and kept my pain hidden from her.

Once the staples were gone, I gave a great sigh of relief and started to make my way home again. Over the next few weeks Graham, and the club's sports scientist Adam Owen, worked on trying to gain as much movement as possible from my knee. I believe they both found it a challenge! Gordon Strachan would occasionally pop his head round the corner to see what all the shouting and screaming was and told me, in his usual dry manner, to keep the noise down as he was trying to watch telly whilst on a long jog on the treadmill. Gordon always managed to raise a smile from me, which helped distract me from the task in hand. During my 12 months of constant physio at Celtic I shared the gym with those players who were also on long-term re-cuperation; Shaun Maloney and John Kennedy. John's will and determination to get back to full fitness and playing again was a huge source of inspiration.

Here was a guy with the world at his feet until it was dragged away from him on his full Scotland debut against Romania when Ionel Ganea basically shattered his knee in what was a shocking and reckless tackle. John had been through many surgeries like myself and was still many months away from playing again. Looking back, I believe he had every confidence in his own determination to get back playing. He worked every day for eight hours, building up his strength and carrying out exercises on his injured knee. When he played again I was thrilled for him, as were many at the football club at the time, but it came as no surprise when he broke down after moving to Norwich on loan. His knee was very badly damaged in that tackle and it's a miracle he has some sort of normal function, never mind playing professional football again. I have nothing but the utmost respect for him. Shaun was the same; his hard work and determination got him back playing at the very highest level – a top lad!

There were many others that came and went, like Craig Beattie who appeared to be always injured. In my opinion, he could have been one of Scotland's finest strikers had he stayed injury-free. Big Adam Virgo, who only played a handful of games for Celtic, was another whose hard work in the gym paid off. Adam and I hit it off from day one, a lovely big guy who never made the grade at Celtic after his big move from Brighton but I am thrilled to see him doing so well now as a pundit on BT Sport. I always believed he would make an excellent pundit after a guest appearance on the *Daily Huddle* following a Man of the Match performance against Motherwell the previous Saturday. Delighted for him!

This brings me nicely to the one player I hoped I could have had some sort of relationship with but due to his demeanour, character, arrogance, and if I'm being honest – worldwide fame – it was never going to happen. Whilst lying in my hospital bed the day after my surgery I sneaked my phone into the ward so I could talk to my family and friends. As I was drifting off to sleep my phone buzzed and it was a message from a football agent friend of mine who told me Roy Keane had just signed for the club and an announcement was due shortly. I had to look at the message twice. Prior to this there had been much speculation in the press that Gordon Strachan was targeting the former Manchester United skipper to bolster his midfield, although Gordon gave nothing away during our interviews.

I had first met Roy during my days at MUTV but found him unfriendly so never really bothered with him; I felt it was best to leave him to his own devices. I did interview him for an analysis show we recorded every Monday morning at the Carrington Studios where a selected player would look back at the weekend's game. It just so happened that Roy was down to be interviewed the Monday after he was sent off against Newcastle in a heavy defeat which saw him lash out at Alan Shearer. As I sat with the production team outside the small studio, we discussed intently whether he would show up? To his credit, he did.

This was the first time I had been in his company and I tried to make small talk before we started recording, but he was not interested in anything I had to say. To lighten the mood I decided to play him at his own game and discover whether he had a sense of humour. During the show, when we looked back on the incident with Alan Shearer, Roy offered a very honest and well thought-out answer. I then asked him why, if he tried to punch Alan Shearer, he didn't do it properly as during the skirmish he missed! Thankfully, this raised a smile from the Irishman and he seemed to lighten up. It worked. After the show I offered him my hand and thanked him for his time; he just smiled and shook my hand without saying a word.

During my time with MUTV I saw him on numerous

occasions but he did very little to engage me, even when prompted. I have been brought up to always say good morning, afternoon or evening and to offer politeness, even when it's not offered back. It was seldom offered from Mr Keane. When he signed for Celtic it was front-page news in Scotland. Everybody in the office was incredibly excited; the fans were delighted, even though some hardened souls questioned his fitness and reasoning. Had he come just to fulfil a schoolboy dream? I did wonder, the morning I made my way to the ground, whether he would remember me and stop to say hello? Who was I kidding! As I stood in my usual spot chatting to the receptionist, Roy walked in, met my eye, nodded his head and walked on by.

I chuckled to myself. When he injured himself it was the same time I was going hell for leather with my own recuperation. As I worked hard on the bike to keep the flexibility in my knee at a good level, I could sense he was not best pleased I was sharing the gym with him. I asked Graham and Roddy if it was OK to be there and they both told me not to worry and crack on, but in all honesty – in hindsight – I should have packed up for the day and hit the showers. As I always did in the gym, if I was in the company of the players, I did my best to mind my own business and not disturb them in any way.

Thankfully, most of the players were very chatty and always had time for a natter. On the odd occasion that Roy and I shared the gym I kept well out his way; I always offered a smile and a hello, as I did to all players, but more times than not I received a grunt in return. When he played he made little impact on the club, he was quite clearly struggling with his injuries and not 100% fit. I was not overly bothered when he retired.

In conclusion, Roy Keane on the pitch is undoubtedly one of the greatest; if you asked me to pick my top five he would be in it. A machine that led with his heart on his sleeve, I admired his honesty in interviews and his auto-biography is one of the best football books I have read. I have interviewed him twice, once at MUTV, once at Celtic. He is fascinating to interview, always ready with an honest answer, he never shirks from telling the truth or what he believes; frankly, he can be a breath of fresh air! When the cameras are off though, I was always left disappointed. He is what he is, accept it and crack on, or continually be left to feel disappointment. In all honesty, with the power of hindsight, I couldn't care less now; he's just a human being like the rest of us after all!

I continued to have phsyio at Celtic up until the day I left. Like Graeme Souness, Dave Fevre and the staff at Blackburn, I owe a huge debt of gratitude to Roddy McDonald, Graham, Adam and Gordon for allowing me to use the facilities at Celtic Park and get the benefit of their impressive expertise. I don't know why I have been so fortunate to receive such luck.

That good fortune began during the early days of the band when, due to our rigorous dance moves, I found myself with troubled quadriceps. The problem escalated after a few months due to our busy schedule and I found myself unable to fulfil the choreographed routines. I had not long started playing football for the Arsenal celebs when I called Alan Sefton at Arsenal and asked for his help. Alan put me in touch with first-team physiotherapist Gary Lewin. Gary invited me down to Highbury, so after a photoshoot round the corner in Islington, our driver kindly whisked me off to the famous old ground and my first encounter with a man who would become one of my fondest friends, not that I knew it at the time!

Gary greeted me at the steps of the players' entrance and I marvelled at the Art Deco style building. I had been to Highbury a couple of times to watch Arsenal but never had I stepped foot inside the main entrance. The bust of Herbert Chapman dominates it and I felt very privileged, all of a sudden, to be there. Gary greeted me like a lost friend and led me into the home dressing room. The heated marble floors impressed me from the off, the huge players' bath, the individual player baths and, of course, the dressing area itself. Here I was standing in the middle of a room where so many great players had sat and graced the place with their presence. Gary took me into his room where all sorts of medical equipment dominated the small area. He told me to strip off, and threw me a pair of Arsenal shorts, which I took to like a kid to chocolate.

I knew it was just a pair of shorts but anybody could have worn them; Tony Adams, Ian Wright, maybe Paul Merson? I was a little bit excited! Gary asked me to sit on the bed and examined my thighs. He placed what looked like some sort of heat sensor on my thigh and started to rub some sticky stuff into my leg. It was actually quite re-freshing, even if I say so myself! He told me I had strained both thigh muscles and needed to rest. I told him, that due to the schedule of the band, this was impossible. He asked me what sort of footwear I was wearing on stage and it just so happened that I was wearing my old military boots that very day. Gary took one look at them and said they had to go!

Gary did not mess about. He told me I needed support and this started with proper footwear. He wanted me to rest, first and foremost, so the quadriceps had time to heal. He gave me a list of instructions and told me to call him in a month to see how I was progressing. Over the next few years, Gary treated all my football injuries, from breaking my foot to the beginnings of a serious knee problem. I could call him at any time of the day and, if he could, he would always gladly treat me. Not once did he ever ask for payment or favours but I did my best to make sure his children got the very best seats at a Robbie Williams concert once!

I was delighted when he was offered the England job; he is an outstanding physio and deserved his place on Team England. More recently, I required more surgery after my knee started to give me many problems after moving to Singapore. I managed, with the help of ESPN, to gain a new set of X-rays and MRI scans. Gary was quick to tell me, upon receipt of the scans, that more surgery would be needed to fix a number of problems developing in my knee. I decided a trip home for a couple of weeks were required. Gary organised for me to visit Dr John King at the London Independent Hospital in south London. Dr King explained a number of concerns and said it was imperative that he operated sooner rather than later. Two days later I found myself once again lying in a hospital bed answering questions to a host of nurses, giving blood samples and fasting, the one part I really dislike about surgery!

After the surgery was complete I was able to fly home to Aberdeen where I stayed with Mum for a week or two. Prior to the op, I had spoken to Dave Wylie at Aberdeen and asked for his help. Dave has been the club's physio for over 25 years. He was more than willing to offer his services. Physiotherapy is not easy; it can be a long painful road where patience, a strong will and plenty of determination is required. Thankfully, after the surgery, my knee was able to take my full weight but I had to be careful! My knee felt very vulnerable to the point where I was almost a little paranoid! Dave tested my will to the maximum! In a perverse kind of way I was looking forward to attending Pittodrie and seeing some of my old friends and allowing Dave to work away on my knee.

Nothing prepared me for the initial shock of horrific pain that hit me when Dave began his plan of treatment. He decided, first and foremost, not to allow any scar tissue to develop in and around my incisions. Trust me when I say I was a little perturbed when he slipped on a pair of rubber gloves! I did wonder what sort of treatment he was about to offer! He told me to lie back, take a deep breath in, and let it out. As I exhaled he rammed his finger into my incision, which was still healing and proceeded to rub vigorously back and forward. Well, I just about hit the ceiling, swore a few times and did my best not to punch him! Dave couldn't have cared less; he knew exactly what he was doing and, more importantly, why he was doing it!

Over the years I've been through an assortment of pain from the early days when Dave Fevre was manipulating my knee, to Graham and Adam at Celtic pushing my leg towards my bottom to try and gain more movement. But these sessions in the bowels of Pittodrie were the worst! The pain was horrific, the incision started to bleed but I could feel the tissue breaking and softening. Dave's expertise was obviously rubbing off (excuse the pun) but as I looked at him for some sort of relief, he just smiled and told me to stop being a wimp! He continued this course of treatment for the next few minutes while I did my best to control my breathing.

I was getting hot and the sweat started to form round my brow. I was hurting and hurting badly! After what seemed like an age, Dave told me to rest while he worked on my ankle and lower limbs. I was ready to pass out! Dave worked on my knee every second day for two weeks. Neil Simpson made the occasional appearance to see how things were going. I'm convinced he, like many of my friends at Pittodrie, found a small amount of amusement in my uncomfortable state. Zander Diamond popped in now and then to see how I was progressing, as did Fraser Fyvie. As the treatment neared the end I could feel a marked improvement. My muscles felt stronger in both my thigh and lower leg and the pain had eased considerably.

I am indebted to Dave for his help; he was great company and quite obviously an expert in his field. He is part of the make-up at Pittodrie; some may argue he's part of the bricks and mortar. Alongside John Sharp, they make a great team and the players are fortunate to have such experts looking after them. We talk often and I look forward to the day when I see him again. Unfortunately, my knee continues to give me problems, which requires further surgery, but I'm sure it would have deteriorated even further if it wasn't for the help of Dave over that two-week period. This is just a personal thought, if anybody at Aberdeen FC deserves a testimonial it is Dave Wylie. I hope the club, and the board, recognise his service over the years and do the right thing by him.

At the time of writing, I am waiting to have more surgery after my knee deteriorated even further. As before, Gary Lewin and Dave Fevre offered me the best advice possible and I am indebted to them both for their support and friendship. One day my right knee will be replaced, I am looking forward to that day like none other; to have some sort of normality back, be pain free, and kick a ball about with Lennox is my own personal goal. It will be a great day when it happens!

From the East End of Glasgow ...
to the Far East

In 2007, just two months after my Dad died, I accepted a new job with ESPN Star Sports based in Singapore. Having worked with Setanta and Celtic TV for four years I felt the time was right for a new challenge. I feared for Setanta, as much as I was astonished at their progress as a serious sports broadcaster. Buying all the rights for various sports to compete, largely with Sky, was bold, if not slightly reckless. Setanta had financial backing from various institutions but had nowhere near the subscription levels needed to support the vast amounts of capital they were spending on securing rights.

I applauded their ambition and fortitude, but feared for their future too as I did those who I'd formed strong bonds with over the years. Their platform was impressive; strong production coupled with established broadcasters meant Sky was given a good run for their money. But, Setanta sprinted before they could crawl and their over-ambitious executives ultimately cost the company its place in the market. Thankfully, I managed to jump ship before it well and truly sank.

I am extremely lucky and fortunate to have a job that I truly love. I very much doubt many people can actually say that, but the television industry, very much like its music counterpart, is brutal! The industry is full of numpties who believe the whole world revolves around them. If you have any ambition of working in the television industry you have to be prepared to work with people whose egos, at times, can be overbearing. Now that I am in a senior position my man-management skills have been tested to their absolute limit but I believe this has strengthened my own character and improved my working relations with people. I have been accused on more than one occasion by the weak of raising my voice and swearing while producing shows. I ashamedly confess this is true and quickly learnt from a cultural point of view that this type of behaviour is frowned upon. A happy and efficient television gallery is a calm gallery. I now only raise my voice to convey clear and precise instructions and the use of bad language is saved for days at Pittodrie!

For any television executive reading these pages I would like to make one very simple request. Please return people's emails. Budding presenters, producers, directors etc have taken the time and courage to touch base with you to try and help them forge a career in the industry. I can't express how disappointing it is when an executive can't be bothered to reply. I have been there a thousand times and trust me when I tell you it's soul-destroying not to mention downright rude! I can take a rejection anytime but to be snubbed or dismissed out of hand without rebuttal is infuriating. I recall a friend of mine who was heading up a shopping channel out of London and threw a CD of someone's showreel into his bin without even looking at it. His behaviour that day enraged me and I had no fear in telling him so! Some poor sod had spent time editing that reel, finding my mate's contact details, and sending the reel at his or her expense hoping that maybe, just maybe my mate would touch base and offer them a chance of forging a career in television!

Unfortunately, it's part of life working in my industry, but the rewards far outweigh the negative aspects to the job. My job is incredibly rewarding. Every day is different, my job brings new challenges and new hurdles but the satisfaction I receive from producing live football almost makes up for not making it as a professional. I made a decision, after producing the London 2012 Olympic Games; I will never present again. My career in front of the camera is over but reaching that decision meant more soul-searching. In May 2009, after two very successful years presenting for ESPN Star Sports, I fully expected my contract to be renewed. All the signs pointed towards another term with the company and all feedback received was tremendously encouraging. The last thing I expected when I sat down with my boss was to be told that he was letting me go due to my Scottish accent. I was stunned! It turned out the managing director, Manu Sawney, did not like my accent and cited problems understanding me. I requested a meeting with the MD but was flatly turned down. Sawney took the cowardly route, he instructed someone else to do his dirty work, the worst kind of person in my book. When he left the company in 2012 not many tears were shed in the office.

At the time I was appalled and felt very much betrayed but in an ironic twist of fate, with the benefit of hindsight, it is probably the best thing that has ever happened to me. My head of production at ESPN, Huw Bevan, gave me an opportunity to step into production and learn a whole new career. I took up the challenge and threw myself in. Sports production can be incredibly rewarding, the buzz you can get from producing live events is like nothing else, even more so than performing in front of 100,000 screaming girls.

Many people over the years have asked me for my opinion on what makes a good presenter. As a producer, I am able to appreciate more how difficult the job actually is and the volume of support a presenter needs from his/her producer. A good presenter is one who has unlimited knowledge of the subject matter. Too many modern day presenters are employed for their looks and not talent. I get it, but it doesn't mean I have to agree with it. A presenter's role is to guide the show along seamlessly, to get from A to B from B to C, and so on.

A sports presenter is one who loads the gun for their guests to fire. Pundits are there for a reason, to offer expert opinion and analysis. A bad presenter is one who loves the sound of his/her own voice and offers an opinion or two more than they should. If a presenter has played a particular sport to the very highest level, and by that I mean professionally and not just down the park with their mates, they are entitled to a personal opinion. They have earned the right to do so. As I mentioned in a previous chapter, all presenters should have the ability to ad-lib and not read from an autocue. All presenters should be able to take instruction from their producers and studio directors without fuss. But most importantly, all presenters must have the ability to remain calm when the shit hits the fan.

Living in Singapore meant new and uncharted ways to follow the Dons; which brings me nicely to social media, and the dangerous game we all play! I thank Malcolm Panton and his staff in the media department at Aberdeen FC for having the foresight to set up an internet club channel. Red TV is an excellent platform to keep up-to-date with all the news coming out of Pittodrie. As a fan living and working abroad, it means I can watch the odd live game and all the highlights from the weekend's matches, albeit in the middle of the night.

Social media has become a global phenomenon. All clubs have seen the future; it is, without a shadow of doubt, the way forward. We can now even watch a live match while flying, or taking a holiday on a cruise liner. Whatever next! Where I believe social media has fallen down is with our national sport, and the progress of our youngsters. For many years, experts have debated at all levels the reasons why Scotland, as a nation, does not produce great players anymore. I mean this with the greatest respect to all our current national players, but name me one player in the mould of a Graeme Souness, Kenny Dalglish, Billy Bremner, Jimmy Johnstone, Willie Miller, Jim Baxter, Danny McGrain, Alex McLeish or Denis Law! We, as a nation, with the greatest will in the world, do not produce – why?

The coaching system is in place. The Scottish Football Association could not do more in terms of education, practice and delivery. Coaching courses are regularly available where qualifications can be achieved, which means coaching can be delivered to all levels of society. I am of the opinion that youngsters today are more interested in playing football on their PlayStation or X-Box. Society has changed, I defy any parent not to feel slightly unnerved when their youngsters disappear for hours on end without contact. When I grew up, I was actively encouraged to disappear for most of the day! Kids these days would rather Facebook or tweet than physically have a game of football down the local park with their mates. No wonder we don't produce! I do wish that someone, somewhere, would grab this problem by the balls and do something about it for the sake of our treasured game!

Moving on now that I have clambered down from my high horse! What I never expected in all my years as a fan was a time when I actually felt like giving up on the Dons. That came only two months after the incredible run in the Europa League. Against all the odds, Aberdeen qualified for the last 32 by beating FC Copenhagen at Pittodrie in the final group game. I watched on from my apartment in Singapore not quite knowing what to do with myself. As the goals rained in against the shell-shocked Danes, I danced round the place like some sort of crazed lunatic. My energy levels and adrenaline keeping me awake at 5am! Here I was re-enacting my childhood, yet this time as an adult.

My demeanour and comical celebration at the age of 37 was just like that of myself as a child. It's what I love about football – it brings the kid out in you! Maybe my feelings at the time bordered on the childish, but I was so disillusioned with what was unfolding in front of me that I almost couldn't help myself. Aberdeen had reached the semi-finals of the Scottish Cup by beating Celtic in a replay at Celtic Park, thanks to a solitary goal by Darren Mackie. In the first leg at Pittodrie, a last-gasp equaliser denied the Dons. I was on air at the time and it took all my professionalism not to show my emotions. I believed our chance had gone! When Darren scored what proved to be the winner I was already planning a trip home for the final, surely the Dons could get past Queen of the South!

For the semi-final my former boss in the football department at ESPN organised for the Aberdeen versus Queen of the South Scottish Cup semi-final to be fed into the office via our various satellite links. The players that day embarrassed themselves with a performance that should never be replicated by any Dons team – ever! If running out at Hampden in front of a capacity crowd for a Scottish Cup Final is not a big enough incentive then they shouldn't be playing the game. As a fan, I find it almost incomprehensible that the players allowed a performance like that to be played out over 90 minutes.

I take nothing away from the Queen of the South players,

who played like warriors that day. They fought for every ball, closed the Dons down, and had the bravery to take the game to them without fear. They thoroughly deserved their place in the final. The Queens players knew this was their big chance at glory. Here was a team full of part-timers, who displayed more grit and determination than any of the full-time professionals wearing the red shirts. It was a shameful day and I believe this abject performance was the beginning of the end for Jimmy Calderwood as Aberdeen manager.

After the game, I set about preparing for another busy show but felt lost in my thoughts. For the first time since becoming a fan I contemplated giving up on the Dons. I was hurting like never before; here was a game where the final was almost handed to them on a plate. I struggled to understand how, bar one or two changes from the Copenhagen game, the side managed to put on such contradicting performances? I knew deep down such thoughts should be banished and no matter what you should support your team through thick and thin, the good and the bad times, but this was almost unbearable. The players were not deserving of my support after that game, why should I give them everything emotionally when they offer little back? I confess, for two to three weeks I stayed away from all things Dons.

But, being the type of fan I am, it wasn't long before I was back. I knew a big game against Rangers on the final day was just around the corner and a win would mean fourth spot, but more importantly hand Celtic the league title! The night we beat Rangers to stop them winning the title, I rediscovered my passion for the Dons and bore feelings of such guilt that I had even considered deserting them. The Dons finished the season on a high, a season, which like so many before them offered all Dons fans an emotional rollercoaster of a ride. We had been teased, even tormented. Dare I say it, but it felt like the good ol' days!

When Jimmy Calderwood left, I couldn't help but feel a degree of sympathy towards him. He had done so much to restore the club's place in the SPL. Of course, Aberdeen is in no position to challenge for the league and won't for many, many years to come but with the help of Sandy Clark and Jimmy Nicholl between them, they restored some sort of parity. Unfortunately for Jimmy, I believe his legacy will be the shocking manner in which the Dons submitted to Queen's Park and Queen of the South in the League and Scottish Cups, respectively. The fine Europa League campaign, and famous victories over both sides of the Old Firm had almost been forgotten due to these unforgivable losses. Looking back, I think his sacking was a season premature. Willie Miller and the board should have given him one more shot. Who knows, with the right resources, what Jimmy could have achieved? Alas, we will never know. For me, he was a resounding success.

I will always be grateful to him for taking the time to do a phone interview with me for my news show on Star Sports on the morning after the night before, when the lads thumped FC Copenhagen. I could hear the pride in his voice, the excitement of taking the Dons into uncharted waters. Like so many Dons managers before him, Jimmy deserves his place in the history books. Whenever I'm home, I like nothing more than to pop into Pittodrie and catch up with old friends for a good blether. Malcolm Panton and I have become solid pals over the years and he knows I need no invitation to drop down for a spot of lunch in the staff canteen and play a game of spot the player! I always take the opportunity to watch the lads train. To observe them at close quarters is fascinating stuff.

I like nothing more than to take a moment to myself, lose myself in my thoughts and watch on quietly as the boys go about their set pieces and training drills.

Malcolm has very kindly interviewed me once or twice for RED TV, talking about days gone by. I like nothing more than waxing lyrical about the Dons! On one occasion Malcolm sat me down in the Gothenburg suite to conduct an interview. Once we concluded, I asked him if I could have my picture taken with the Cup Winners' Cup. "No problem," Malcolm said and duly marched me round to the boardroom where in front of me, in pride of place was the cup itself!

I took a hold of it and held it close. I can't really explain on paper what that moment felt like. I was a little overcome if I'm honest. Here was the very same trophy that had given me one of my fondest moments in life, a trophy that played a major role in my youth and upbringing. A trophy that had cost Dad a small fortune but yet, like me, given him an unforgettable night. That moment was special. Malcolm told me to strike the Willie Miller pose, which I did. I love that picture and spent a good hour in the boardroom scanning over the various photographs and artefacts that neatly occupy the room.

It was round about this time former Aberdeen striker Mark McGhee was named manager. I had mixed feelings about Mark's appointment. Here was an Aberdeen legend that knew the club inside out, and what the fans expected, but I had reservations about his track record as a manager. He was doing very well at Motherwell but was it enough? Like many others, I was willing to give Mark the benefit of the doubt but he did not exactly endear himself to the fans when he said in his first press conference he would rather have had the Celtic job. In my opinion he was doomed before he even started!

Mark's tenure in charge was nothing short of a disaster. He got off to the worst possible start in the Europa League qualifier with a shocking 5–1 defeat at Pittodrie against unknown Sigma Olomouc. Aberdeen, that night, were bereft of ideas and looked so far out their depth it was frightening to watch. It didn't get any better from there on in. Truly awful defeats against lower league opposition in both cup competitions meant a throwback to Jimmy Calderwood's days. Surely lightning won't strike twice? For the next 18 months, I watched on from afar incredulous of Mark's tactics and post-match reactions. With all due respect to him, I sensed he was in denial of what was going on around him. The football on display was nothing short of abject. Aberdeen had lost their way in spectacular fashion and it all came to a head at Celtic Park.

The 6th November 2010 is a date all Aberdeen fans should cast aside; it should not be spoken of again. I was a year into my wonderful relationship with my then girlfriend, and now wife, Miriam. Miriam was starting to understand my passion for this football team from the north-east of Scotland. She watched on with a degree of bemusement, it has to be said, at my erratic behaviour whilst watching the Dons on my PC. Not being a football fan, she struggled at times to understand what was going on in my head and why I allowed this team to dictate my emotions over a 90-minute period. Being from Austria, but with an excellent understanding of the English language she did, at times, struggle to understand my rants and raves. I think she found the arm-waving and loud exhales a particular source of amusement.

After an evening on the town and the odd "radler", or shandy as it's more commonly known in English, I asked Miriam modestly "if I rub your feet can I watch the Aberdeen game?" I had tried this tactic before and it seemed to work with little objection from Mrs Begg so we settled down with foot in hand and laptop at the ready. Miriam did ask me if I was sure I wanted to watch the game, maybe she was already growing a sixth sense! I simply tutted and started to massage! Like all Aberdeen fans, I'm sure all I was hoping for ahead of kick-off was for the Dons to keep it tight in the opening period, don't allow Celtic to take control and maybe once or twice hit them on the counter-attack. For the first 26 minutes I was surprisingly upbeat, Miriam was in heaven! Then it all fell apart in the most spectacular way possible. When Anthony Stokes opened the scoring I was OK, when Celtic scored their second only two minutes later I was deflated. "Oh well, game over," I said to Miriam.

When Gary Hooper scored a third on 33 minutes I was now pissed off, the foot rubbing becoming more vigorous and aggressive. Miriam loved it! The fourth goal was met with a loud "oh, for fuck sake" which startled Miriam. I apologised like a scolded schoolboy and offered to make her a cup of tea. Alone in the kitchen I ranted about the Dons' first-half performance. My dog Casper looked up at me with comical tilt of head wondering why I was talking to myself in such a manner. I feared for the second half. Then the text messages started to arrive. "Ha bleeding ha," I thought as my mates enjoyed a laugh at my expense. Not the first time, and no doubt it won't be the last!

As I returned to the bedroom Miriam asked me if I was sure I wanted to watch the second half. She said to me; "Why do you do it to yourself, they're crap." I laughed at the innocent yet thoughtful quip. Now she was starting to get it! With left foot well and truly rubbed I began on the right as the second half began. Surely the lads could do better, damage limitation from here on in? "Do yourselves proud?" I said out loud thumping fist on chest.

Pride was obviously a word lost on those 11 players who donned the red and white shirt that miserable day in the east end of Glasgow. Mark McGhee looked like a man hoping the Celtic Park ground would swallow him up at any moment as he watched on bereft of ideas. Goal after goal rained down on the Dons. By now, the massaging had stopped in fear of doing some lasting damage. Thankfully, Miriam had fallen asleep as I watched on not quite believing what was unfolding in front of my own eyes. I had to pinch myself a couple of times to really fathom what I was watching. As much as I wanted to turn it off, I was transfixed. When the ninth goal went in, I couldn't take much more, that's when the text messages started again! People I hadn't heard from in a while, colleagues, friends and family, all adding to the misery. As I lay in bed I tried to put the game, and the embarrassment, behind me. It was only a football match after all but this was a sore one.

I continued to be the butt of many jokes for a few days, a particular favorite being "nein" due to my lovely partner and new-found skill of speaking the German language. When the Dons faced Inverness Caley Thistle in the next game I am ashamed to say I hoped they would lose. In all my years as a Dons fan never had I wanted them to actually lose a game but Mark McGhee's clueless reign had to come to an end before serious damage was done. I felt sad. I had delivered a betrayal to the club I loved and it made me sick to the stomach. This is not what I was about and should never have allowed myself to have such negative feelings but I was despairing. Having lost the game 2–1 after leading, I hoped to read news of McGhee's sacking but it didn't materialise for another three games!

With the Dons perilously close to the relegation zone, the board had no choice but to sack Mark, and his assistant Scott Leitch, who I am yet to hear a good word about! I had every confidence the board had the foresight to appoint a coach with a proven track record, a coach who had the experience to grab the players by the scruff of their necks and give them a bloody good shake. In my opinion they did just that! I first met former Scotland manager Craig Brown at my grandpa's funeral way back in 1990. He paid his respects privately, first, before taking time to talk to my family. He put his arm round my shoulder and told me what a great man my grandpa was. He took a few minutes to comfort my gran, and my uncle who was inconsolable at losing his father. I never forgot his kindness. Fast forward a few years when Craig was in charge of Preston. Dad was in Manchester on business and we arranged to take a drive up the motorway to visit Craig at Deepdale. We had a quick walk around the very impressive football museum before meeting Craig for lunch.

We chatted for a while and he told me how he had followed my career since breaking through on MUTV. I had no idea he watched the channel but quickly realised he used it as a tool to watch the live reserve games! We spent a fine hour in his company enjoying his stories. It would be a few years before we bumped into each other again. During my spell with Setanta, the company gained the rights to a host of European leagues including the Dutch Eredivisie, Portugal's Primeira Liga and the German Bundesliga. I was asked to step in to host the coverage until a full-time presenter came on board. It was not unusual for Craig to be one of my guests, alongside Uefa correspondent Alex O'Henley.

Craig's incredible knowledge of all things football was invaluable during the shows. I could throw a simple question at him and he would own the camera for the next few minutes. He was a joy to have around; we spoke often about my grandpa, Aberdeen and life in general. When he was appointed Dons' boss I was over the moon. It was obvious to all Craig required time to sort the club out and I believe, during his tenure, he worked wonders with very little resources at his disposal. The manner of the cup defeats in his first season, though, were difficult to stomach; I honestly don't know how players capitulate so easily in a semi-final. I've mentioned before, the incentive to walk out at Hampden for a major final surely is enough for the lads to go that extra mile but once again the Dons inexplicably surrendered to Celtic on both occasions.

Craig came out and offered his apologies to the fans immediately for the lack of performance. His honesty was a breath of fresh air. He knew he had a serious job on his hands; I for one supported him 100% during his time at the club and believe he set strong foundations for Derek McInnes to take forward. To bring this book to its conclusion, I struggled for a number of weeks to find an apt ending. I wanted to offer some quotes, or list my top ten favourite moments as a Dandy Don. I wrote and rewrote the ending many times. It was becoming a battle until one day, whilst sitting at my desk at work, an unexpected email popped into my inbox from Kevin Stirling, Aberdeen's historian and author of many a fine book.

As I read his email it took me a second or two to take in what Kevin was requesting. In his email he told me he'd received an email from a sports writer called Rob Roberston at *The Daily Mail*. Rob was co-writing Willie Miller's new book where Willie named his all-time Aberdeen XI. Rob had asked if I would like to contribute to Willie's book by naming my own all-time Aberdeen XI. I read the email three times over to make sure what I was reading was actually there in black and white!

This may sound a tad odd to some, but I had to take a walk to comprehend what had just happened. For someone like me, whose life in some small way has been shaped by Aberdeen Football Club, to be asked to compile such a thing is an honour. I tried to explain to you my feelings when I held the Cup Winners' Cup for the first time, I was lost for words. Rob's request was lost on me, and I can't find the words to describe how I felt at that moment. Willie Miller has been my hero for over 30 years, meeting him for the first time at Pittodrie during my spell with the boy band, and having a kick-about on the park, was the stuff of dreams. At the time, life could not have been better. When he surprised me with a birthday wish when my good friend Nick Cochrane and I hosted Talksport in the summer of 2002, I was so excited to hear from him I was unable to get any words out, much to the amusement of Nick and the show's producers.

I immediately phoned Miriam and told her the incredible news; she was so pleased for me even though Aberdeen FC is still very much new to her. I called my brother Peter, who was beside himself with excitement and proceeded to tell me who I should have in my team! And lastly, I called Mum and shared my news. Mum was a little overcome, as she knew what this gesture meant to me. She also said to me how proud Dad would have been. This made me stop and think for a moment about him and how pleased he would be. I can picture him now, sat in his small office in front of his PC with the cat on his lap grinning away at my news.

From page 249 below is the team I selected for Willie's book. I asked BBC broadcaster and fellow Aberdeen fan, Richard Gordon, himself a contributor to Willie's book, for his advice as the last thing I wanted to do was make a tit of myself with my XI and writing. I believe Richard found this all a little amusing but I tried to explain what this meant to me and he kindly looked over my writing for me. Here my book ends, with my own Aberdeen Dream Team XI, which was published in Willie's own book. This book has been a labour of love; I started writing it in the summer of 2003 to give myself something to do whilst recovering from breaking my leg. It's been tough, and at the same time incredibly therapeutic. I have released much stored anger and frustration over the boy band and poured my heart out to you about that whole experience.

If I may be so bold as to use a song title from my boy band days, there IS More To This World than boy bands, celebrity, fame, money, diva TV presenters and executives and discriminating MDs. I don't feel the need to prove myself anymore, I don't need to prove people wrong, I don't have to justify myself to anybody. I'm happy with me and what I've achieved. I am grateful for the help along the way, and the guidance of many. As I bring this book to its conclusion I am a year into a new and exciting job with beIN Sports, based in Doha, Qatar. It's another chapter in my life, another journey, and I face it without prejudice or apprehension. Working closely with Richard Keys, Andy Gray and Angus Scott has elevated my skills as a producer to levels which I wondered if I would ever reach. These guys have opened my eyes to what it takes to make the best football shows out there. I am delighted to be working with them.

All I know is that from my experiences I am a much better and wiser person. I am still very proud to say that from all boy bands of the early 1990s, I am the only one to have forged a successful television-broadcasting career and, to date, the only lad from Scotland to be a member of a relatively successful boy band from this era.

To conclude, I am extremely fortunate and quite obviously blessed to have led the type of life I have. Miriam and I wed in Salzburg, Austria in the summer of 2011 and recently celebrated the birth of our baby son Lennox Mika. When I met her, Miriam gave me a purpose; she put the smile back on my face when faced with adversity after I was removed from my presenting role with ESPN Star. Miriam has loved me and encouraged me throughout. Now that we have Lennox in our lives, I have another purpose. Aberdeen, though, will continue to play a role in my life and hopefully one day, his. I have given my life to Aberdeen; I could not think of a more apt hobby than that bloody football club. If Aberdeen FC were the devil, I sold my soul a million times over!

Aberdeen "Dream Team" XI

Theo Snelders

Stewart McKimmie   Alex McLeish   Willie Miller   Doug Rougvie

Gordon Strachan   Scott Severin   Neil Simpson   Peter Weir

Eoin Jess

Frank McDougall

1. I was torn between Theo Snelders and Jim Leighton. Jim is without question Scotland's finest ever goalkeeper but I opted for Theo for one reason. His penalty shoot-out save from Anton Rogan against Celtic in the 1990 Scottish Cup is the greatest save I have witnessed live.

2. Stewart McKimmie was a simple choice. He epitomised everything a full-back should be; great going forward, superb positional sense, and defended like his life depended on it.

3. Doug Rougvie was an interesting one. Unconventional, and at times a little clumsy, but a brilliant defender, who, coupled with his toothless grin and scowl scared most opponents into submission.

4. Scott Severin. I felt he deserved his place in my team as his leadership during some tough times shone through. I have

yet to see a better player in an Aberdeen shirt since the early 1990s.

5. Alex McLeish, simply Aberdeen's greatest centre-back. No argument and a true gentleman.

6. Willie Miller, simply Aberdeen's greatest ever player, no argument. My hero!

7. Gordon Strachan was a genius. His vision, drive and bravery has not been matched since. Great on the ball, cool under pressure, supported the front men and chipped in with the odd goal. The fact that I got to know him well during my days with Setanta Sports confirmed that he's not just a great player, but a great man too.

8. Neil Simpson was Aberdeen's rock in midfield, his unforgiving style coupled with astonishing levels of fitness dragging the Dons through many a game. He went about his job without fuss or complaint, a truly great midfielder.

11. Have Aberdeen possessed a better winger than Peter Weir? His dazzling runs and pinpoint crosses were the stuff of dreams; his left foot possessed nothing but pure magic. As for hero stakes, he came a very close second behind Mr Miller.

10. Eoin Jess, in my opinion is the last of the great youth products, an outstanding attacking midfielder who in my formation is at his most effective playing in the hole behind the lone striker. A player who could readily slip into any position, his skill, range of passing and uncanny knack of scoring spectacular goals has been sorely missed.

9. I toyed for many an hour with my lone striker. Eric Black, Hans Gillhaus, Charlie Nicholas and Frank McDougall all gave me a headache. In the end Frank got the nod. His predatory instincts in front of goal, his ability to hold the ball up, and his physical presence tipped the scale in his favour. If his injuries had not prematurely ended his career I have no doubt Joe Harper's goalscoring record would have been in serious trouble! His impact in less than 60 games I doubt will be seen again.

Manager: Sir Alex Ferguson

It would border on the ridiculous to select anybody else, not just Aberdeen's greatest ever manager but football's greatest ever manager. I have personal reasons for choosing Sir Alex. Many moons ago the former St Mirren chairman Willie Todd phoned my late grandfather (freelance football journalist, John Begg) and asked him for his advice on whom he thought would make an excellent manager. My grandfather gave Mr Todd one name – Alex Ferguson. Sir Alex once told me never to change my broadcasting style, it's the best compliment I am ever likely to receive... apart from when I was told I was a great singer! Aye right!